THE ANNOTATED SHAKESPEARE

Romeo and Juliet

William Shakespeare

Fully annotated, with an Introduction, by Burton Raffel

With an essay by Harold Bloom

THE ANNOTATED SHAKESPEARE

Yale University Press • *New Haven and London*

Designed by Rebecca Gibb
Set in Bembo type by The Composing Room of Michigan, Inc.
Printed in the United States of America by R. R. Donnelley & Sons.

Library of Congress Cataloging-in-Publication Data
Shakespeare, William, 1564–1616.
Romeo and Juliet / William Shakespeare ; fully annotated, with an
introduction by Burton Raffel ;
with an essay by Harold Bloom.
p.   cm. — (The annotated Shakespeare)
Includes bibliographical references.
ISBN 978-0-300-10453-0 (paperbound)
1. Romeo (Fictitious character)—Drama.   2. Juliet (Fictitious character)—
Drama.   3. Verona (Italy)—Drama.   4. Vendetta—Drama.   5. Youth—
Drama.   I. Raffel, Burton.   II. Bloom, Harold.   III. Title.
PR2878.R6R34   2004
822.3'3—dc22
2004002597

A catalogue record for this book is available from the British Library.

10 9 8 7 6 5 4

For my own Juliet: Elizabeth

CONTENTS

About This Book ix

Introduction xv

Some Essentials of the Shakespearean Stage xxix

Romeo and Juliet 1

An Essay by Harold Bloom 195

Further Reading 215

Finding List 223

ABOUT THIS BOOK

Written four centuries ago, in a fairly early form of Modern English, *Romeo and Juliet* is a gorgeously passionate, witty, and complex text. Many of the play's social and historical underpinnings necessarily need, for the modern reader, the kinds of explanation offered in the Introduction. But what needs even more, and far more detailed, explanation are the play's very words. Toward the end of act 1, scene 1, Romeo and his loyal friend, Benvolio (the name means, in Italian, "well loved," just as Romeo's name, in Italian, means "pilgrim"), spar wittily about the nature of love:

> *Benvolio* Alas that love, so gentle in his view,
>   Should be so tyrannous and rough in proof.
> *Romeo*   Alas that love, whose view is muffled still,
>   Should without eyes see pathways to his will.
>   (lines 78–81)

For comprehension of these lines—completely typical of the play's language—the modern reader needs help. In Benvolio's two lines, gentle = courteous, noble

in his view = in his [Cupid's] appearance ("his" frequently
   means "its'")

rough = disagreeable, harsh

in proof = how it turns out/is experienced.

And in Romeo's two lines,

view is muffled still = whose sight is forever/always blinded
without eyes: Cupid is blind

his will = his pleasure, desire.

The modern reader or listener of course will better understand
this brief exchange in context, as the drama unfolds. But without
full explanation of words that have over the years shifted in meaning, neither the modern reader nor the modern listener is likely
to be equipped for full comprehension.

I believe annotations of this sort create the necessary bridges,
from Shakespeare's four-centuries-old English across to ours. The
only "difficult" words I have not explained in this brief passage are
"tyrannous" and "pathways"; the omissions are deliberate. Many
readers new to matters Elizabethan will already understand these
still current, and largely unchanged, words. Some readers, to be
sure, will be able to comprehend unusual, historically different
meanings without glosses. But when it comes to words like
"tyrannous" and "pathways," those who are not familiar with the
modern meaning will easily find clear, simple definitions in any
modern dictionary. And they may be obliged to make fairly fre-
quent use of such a dictionary: there are a good many less familiar
words, in *Romeo and Juliet,* to be found in modern dictionaries

and not glossed here. Yet most readers are not likely to understand Shakespeare's intended meaning, absent such glosses as I here offer. I have followed the same principles in *The Annotated Milton,* published in 1999, and in my annotated edition of *Hamlet,* published (as the initial volume in this series) in 2003. Classroom experience has validated these editions. Classes of mixed upper-level undergraduates and graduate students have more quickly and thoroughly transcended language barriers than ever before. This allows the teacher, or a general reader without a teacher, to move more promptly and confidently to the non-linguistic matters that have made Shakespeare and Milton great and important poets.

It is the inevitable forces of linguistic change, operant in all living tongues, which have inevitably created such wide degrees of obstacles to ready comprehension—not only sharply different meanings, but subtle, partial shifts in meaning that allow us to think we understand when, alas, we do not. Speakers of related languages like Dutch and German also experience this shifting of the linguistic ground. Like early Modern English (ca. 1600) and the Modern English now current, those languages are too close for those who know only one language, and not the other, to be readily able always to recognize what they correctly understand and what they do not. When, for example, a speaker of Dutch says, "Men kofer is kapot," a speaker of German will know that something belonging to the Dutchman is broken ("kapot" = "kaputt" in German, and "men" = "mein"). But without more linguistic awareness than the average person is apt to have, the German speaker will not identify "kofer" ("trunk" in Dutch) with "Körper"—a modern German word meaning "physique, build, body." The closest word to "kofer" in modern German, indeed, is "Scrankkoffer," which is too large a leap for ready comprehension. Speakers of different Romance languages (such as French, Spanish, or Italian), and all other related but not identical tongues, all experience these difficulties, as well as the difficulty of understanding a text written in their own language five, or six, or seven hundred years earlier. Shakespeare's English is not yet so old that it requires, like many historical texts in French and German, or like Old English texts—for example, *Beowulf*—a modern translation. Much poetry evaporates in translation: language is immensely particular. The sheer sound of Dante in thirteenth-century Italian is profoundly worth preserving. So too is the sound of Shakespeare.

I have annotated prosody (metrics) only when it seemed truly necessary or particularly helpful. Readers should have no problem with the silent "e": whenever an "e" is not silent, it is marked "è". The notation used for prosody, which is also used in the explanation of Elizabethan pronunciation, follows the extremely simple form of my *From Stress to Stress: An Autobiography of English Prosody* (see "Further Reading," near the end of this book). Syllables with metrical stress are capitalized; all other syllables are in lowercase letters. I have managed to employ normal Elizabethan spellings, in most indications of pronunciation, but I have sometimes been obliged to deviate, in the higher interest of being understood.

I have annotated, as well, a limited number of such other matters, sometimes of interpretation, sometimes of general or historical relevance, as have seemed to me seriously worthy of inclusion. These annotations have been most carefully restricted: this is not intended to be a book of literary commentary. It is for that reason that the glossing of metaphors has been severely restricted.

There is almost literally no end to discussion and/or analysis of metaphor, especially in Shakespeare. To yield to temptation might well be to double or triple the size of this book—and would also change it from a historically oriented language guide to a work of an unsteadily mixed nature. In the process, I believe, neither language nor literature would be well or clearly served.

Where it seemed useful, and not obstructive of important textual matters, I have modernized spelling, including capitalization. I have frequently repunctuated. Since the original printed texts of *Romeo and Juliet* (there not being, as there never are for Shakespeare, surviving manuscripts) are frequently careless as well as self-contradictory, I have been relatively free with the wording of stage directions – and in some cases have added small directions, to indicate who is speaking to whom. I have made no emendations; I have necessarily been obliged to make choices. Textual decisions have been annotated when the differences between or among the original printed texts seem either marked or of unusual interest.

In the interests of compactness and brevity, I have employed in my annotations (as consistently as I am able) a number of stylistic and typographical devices:

- The annotation of a single word does not repeat that word
- The annotation of more than one word repeats the words being annotated, which are followed by an equals sign and then by the annotation; the footnote number in the text is placed after the last of the words being annotated
- In annotations of a single word, alternate meanings are usually separated by commas; if there are distinctly different ranges of meaning, the annotations are separated by arabic numerals

inside parentheses—(1), (2), and so on; in more complexly worded annotations, alternative meanings expressed by a single word are linked by a forward slash, or solidus: /

- Explanations of textual meaning are not in parentheses; comments about textual meaning are
- Except for proper nouns, the word at the beginning of all annotations is in lower case
- Uncertainties are followed by a question mark, set in parentheses: (?)
- When particularly relevant, "translations" into twenty-first-century English have been added, in parentheses
- Annotations of repeated words are not repeated. Explanations of the first instance of such common words are followed by the sign★. Readers may easily track down the first annotation, using the brief Finding List at the back of the book. Words with entirely separate meanings are annotated only for meanings no longer current in Modern English.

The most important typographical device here employed is the sign ★ placed after the first (and only) annotation of words and phrases occurring more than once. There is an alphabetically arranged listing of such words and phrases in the Finding List at the back of the book. The Finding List contains no annotations but simply gives the words or phrases themselves and the numbers of the relevant act, the scene within that act, and the footnote number within that scene for the word's first occurrence.

INTRODUCTION

Afar more complex drama than it is sometimes thought, *Romeo and Juliet* (1595?) takes its basic story line from Arthur Brooke's long narrative poem, *The Tragical History of Romeus and Juliet* (1562). Shakespeare could not have taken much else: Brooke's poem is written in one of the dullest verse forms in English literary history, Poulter's Measure, being rhymed couplets of alternating hexameter and septameter length. The *Tragical History* makes soporific reading. Yet the source of a plot is no more than a beginning; Shakespeare almost invariably worked from borrowed plots. He could have taken this story line from a good many other sources, for many were readily available; there is convincing evidence, however, that he worked from Brooke alone. Again, what matters most, and what I will discuss here, is what Shakespeare did with his ready-made narrative.

Romeo and Juliet is, first of all, one of the central texts in the long history of Western love stories. How and why one person falls in love with another is obviously, and properly, of primary human concern. Nobel Prize–winner Isaac Bashevis Singer often said that all stories are love stories. "The universal novel of creation," he wrote in *Gifts*, at age eighty-one, "is finally a love story."

And "Romeo" has long since come to mean, in our language, a lover, as well as someone persistently preoccupied with loving.

It is a mistake to believe either that Shakespeare's Romeo is excessively passionate or that he and Juliet are in some way recklessly immature and unthinking. Renaissance (and to a large extent later medieval) approaches to love were founded on two bodily organs, neither of them the brain. The eyes were thought to begin the process. Sight was indeed indispensable, and sight, like the wind and the rain, happens to be a physically based occurrence over which humans have no control. But the eyes alone could not create love. The eyes transmitted the image they saw, automatically and without any notion of preconception or planning, straight into the organs of emotion. Stirred by such a physical impact, the recipient's heart and soul were inevitably and irreversibly bound by that wry, sly, and even malevolent god Love, who was identified with the bow-wielding blind imp, Cupid.

In more physiological terms than the Renaissance usually employed: it was image-carrying light beams that, like Cupid's arrows, were shot into receiving—and to be sure receptive—eyes. These light beams traveled directly and without interruption down into the inner, affective seats of being. (One must fudge a bit, here, since it had not yet been fully settled that the heart was uniquely the center of such matters; the liver and sometimes also the kidneys were still considered relevant.) The many light-oriented metaphors used, first and last, to depict the heroine of Romeo and Juliet fairly leap out at us; their ideational underpinning is a good deal less obvious. It is still less obvious that Juliet, too, sometimes uses light-related metaphors in speaking of Romeo and of their love. Their love, she says, is "Too like the lightning, which doth cease to be / Ere one can say 'It lightens'"

(2.2.119–120). When the Nurse is late returning from her message-bearing visit to Romeo, Juliet declares, "Love's heralds should be thoughts, / Which ten times faster glide than the sun's beams" (2.5.4–5). It is entirely fitting, to be sure, that her love is not depicted in precisely the same terms as his. She can be his sun, moon, and stars, but an Elizabethan woman views her beloved as her "lord." Juliet is crisp and direct, for a Renaissance woman (though no more straightforward than many of Shakespeare's female characters—think of Desdemona, Portia, Cordelia, and the often misunderstood Ophelia). She apologizes to Romeo for her forwardness. Romeo is reverential, gentle, respectful. But he does not apologize for his sweeping passion.

If, as often happens, the lover did not have the same powerful effect on his or her beloved, love was unilateral and largely unsatisfiable. What factors made for receptivity were left vague and largely undiscussed. Love happened, or it did not. The party or parties involved knew with great clarity what they knew, once they had been stricken; nothing else counted. Like so many developments in human existence, life's directions were subject to unknowable forces—destiny, fate, or astrological configurations. Rebellion against such outwardly determined directions was always possible. But not successful: fatalism was not simply another way of looking at life but a recognition of fundamental reality.

Far from being wantons, accordingly, Romeo and Juliet were fortunate to find one another, just as they were unfortunate in other ways. Rosaline—Romeo's unseen, unheard, but often referred to—initial beloved, was to the Renaissance mind someone our hero plainly loved only conceptually, intellectually. That sort of "love" was not and could not be genuine, profound, and soul shaking. Nor was it generally reciprocated. It was a mere game.

People did not trifle or toy with Cupid's unstoppable arrows. They bled from them, which is a very different affair entirely. Love was not to be casually identified with mere happiness.

The comparative youth of Romeo and, especially, of Juliet is yet another non-issue. Count Paris appears to be younger than Romeo, and to my knowledge, no one has ever suggested that his unreciprocated but apparently genuine love for Juliet is in any way immature. The critical focus is of course largely on Juliet, who is not quite fourteen. But not only do human females mature biologically at a much more rapid pace than do human males, they also mature emotionally at roughly corresponding speed. Wives have always tended to be younger than husbands; legal limits on marriageable age (a relatively recent development) tend to recognize and enforce custom. In the southern states of the United States, not so long ago, males were permitted to marry at sixteen, females at fourteen. It is generally accepted that maturation accelerates in warmer climates—and Shakespeare's play is set in Italy. Indeed, Mary Queen of Scots had been married at fifteen. For a marriage to be permissible, in England at that time, the minimal age was "at least 14 for a boy and 12 for a girl."[1] Throughout Europe, indeed, "girls could be betrothed at the age of three, though marriage had to be delayed till twelve. In the fifteenth century a daughter unmarried at fifteen was a family disgrace."[2]

Yet Romeo and Juliet's misfortunes are not caused exclusively by dark, mysterious, and unfathomable powers. Lawrence Stone's analysis of these lovers' downfall does not fully explain the play, but it does highlight a social vector that we in our time often neglect: "To an Elizabethan audience the tragedy of Romeo and Juliet . . . lay not so much in their ill-starred romance as in the way they brought destruction upon themselves by violating the norms of the society in which they lived, which . . . meant strict filial obedience and loyalty to the traditional friendships and enmities of the lineage. An Elizabethan courtier would be familiar enough with the bewitching passion of love to feel some sympathy with the young couple, but he would see clearly enough where duty lay."[3] We may say with equal justice that the "norms" of the society in which these lovers lived, which tolerated (even if they did not encourage) deep and dangerous feuds, brought destruction and death to many more than Romeo and Juliet alone. In the course of the tragedy, Mercutio, Tybalt, and Paris die for exactly the same flawed cause.

Not only is it clear that the Capulets and the Montagues are at fault, but we are given satiric, barbed portraits of the leaders of both families. They are very old, but not remarkably wise, for all their great years. "What noise is this? Give me my long sword, ho!" croaks old Capulet in act 1, scene 1 (line 83). To which senile bravado his wife responds, "A crutch, a crutch! Why call you for a sword?" Capulet persists, seeing old Montague coming, and—to Capulet's mind—"flourish[ing] his blade in spite of me." Montague is no wiser or more mature. "Thou villain Capulet!" he cries, and then, when his wife too attempts to restrain him, he exclaims, "Hold me not, let me go." Lady Montague, womanly more sensible, asserts, "Thou shalt not stir one foot to seek a foe."

In the course of the play, we see more of old Capulet than we do of old Montague, and what we see usually fits the same intemperate, often befuddled initial portrait. Capulet is more mellow, at first, in act 1, scene 5, even urging calm and tolerance on Tybalt. But when Tybalt argues with him, Capulet sputters out an explosively irrational tirade, mixing his invective with staccato comments on and to the dancing guests (lines 76–81, 82–88). Capulet's denunciation of his daughter for refusing to honor her father's plans for her marriage is neither tempered nor sagacious: "Out, you green sickness carrion! Out, you baggage! . . . An you be mine, I'll give you to my friend— / An you be not, hang! Beg! Starve! Die in the streets!" (3.5.156, 192–193). And in act 4, scene 4, just before the discovery of Juliet's "death," Capulet plays the role of an excited, dithering old fellow, far too caught up to display even minimal dignity. "A jealous hood, a jealous hood!" he cackles at his wife, when she assures him that his errant nocturnal amours are over and done with (line 13).

A more trenchant argument based on the prevailing social norms as Shakespeare has chosen to present them would be, in fact, that the upper levels of Verona society are not only at fault but badly in need of reformation. "Capulet, Montague," says the prince, plainly including himself and his reign in the castigation. "See what a scourge is laid upon your hate . . . / And I, for winking at your discords too, / Have lost a brace of kinsmen. All are punished" (5.3.291–294). Verona's citizenry is literally up in arms against violent brawling in its streets. "Down with the Capulets! Down with the Montagues!" (1.1.83). "As much as the deaths of Juliet and her Romeo, so young and so alive," emphasizes Rosalie L. Colie, "the waste of a man like Mercutio cries out for civil settlement of the old men's vendetta."[4]

But the citizenry was not against the wearing of swords by all males of the upper levels ("gentlemen"), nor against the chivalric codes by which fighting among those gentlemen was more or less regulated. Neither, at least in *Romeo and Juliet*, does Shakespeare appear so disposed. Tybalt, negatively portrayed, is trigger-happy, but Mercutio, not far behind in violence and aggression, is presented with magical warmth. So, too, is Romeo, who takes swift and successful revenge on Tybalt, for Mercutio's death, and who reluctantly but efficiently disposes of an angry and violence-hungry Paris. It must be remembered that one of Shakespeare's most important dramatist colleagues, Ben Jonson, wore and on occasion used a sword to settle a quarrel, once killing his antagonist. Jonson claimed gentlemanly status, though in all probability falsely. Another major English dramatist, Christopher Marlowe, was stabbed to death in a tavern brawl, the rights and wrongs of which have never been decisively determined: Marlowe's death may well have been a political assassination. But Marlowe was a university graduate, and thus of undoubted gentlemanly rank. John Day, a distinctly minor playwright but also a university graduate, killed the obscure playwright Henry Porter with his rapier. Shakespeare had no gentlemanly background, but he spent years trying, finally successfully, to obtain (for a price) a gentleman's coat of arms. He was also, on the record, very much occupied with attaining landowner status, yet another gentlemanly attribute.

In short, social hierarchies—which to this day play a large role in Britain—were in Shakespeare's time starkly powerful. "The key symbols of Tudor and Early Stuart society were the hat [which the lower classes had to doff to their betters] and the whip [which the upper classes were entitled to use on their inferiors]. . . . There was even Tudor class legislation about sport, archery being prescribed for the lower orders, and bowls and tennis restricted to gentlemen with an income of over 100 [pounds] a year."[5] The masters commanded; the servants obeyed. "Get me ink and paper / And hire post horses," Romeo orders. His servant, Balthasar, demurs. "I do beseech you, sir, have patience." A wiser servant can thus make what seem to him or her useful suggestions. Romeo pays no heed: "Leave me and do the thing I bid thee do . . . Get thee gone" (5.1.25–27, 30, 32). And Balthasar goes, without another word.

One measure of the Nurse's partially ambivalent class status is precisely the impertinence displayed toward her by her servant, Peter. She does indeed have a servant, which is usually a lady's prerogative, but the Nurse's servant talks back, most casually. "I saw no man use you at his pleasure" (2.4.146). Paris neither expects nor receives such flippancies from his servant. "Give me thy torch, boy. Hence, and stand aloof" (5.3.1). Nor does Romeo indulge his manservant, especially when he is grimly serious. "If thou . . . do return to pry . . . ," he warns Balthasar, "By heaven, I will tear thee joint by joint" (5.3.33–35). We may perhaps doubt, from our twenty-first-century perspective, that Romeo would so assault his servant. But Balthasar quite rightly has no such doubts, knowing that aroused masters could and did do exactly such mayhem. "I dare not," Balthasar tells Friar Laurence, who has requested his companionship in entering the tomb. "My master knows not but I am gone hence, / and fearfully did menace me with death / If I did stay" (5.3.131–134). Not even priestly protection and shielding can persuade him to the contrary. Indeed, one sure sign of the buffoon stature of Petruchio, in *The Taming of the Shrew*, is precisely that, talked back to by a servant, he does not use his sword or his dagger but first argues with the servant, at some length, then performs the commanded act himself, and at last "wrings [the wonderfully insouciant servant] by the ears." The servant cries out for help, as no ordinary servant would even think of doing, and even less typically announces that "My master is mad"— that is, insane (1.2.5–17). It was not then considered a mad act for masters to behave with great violence to their servants. Patricia Fumerton points out that "much evidence points to unsettling relations between servants . . . and their masters. . . . [A]s court records testify, mistreatment and violence . . . were common."[6] Sir William Blackstone's *Commentaries on the Laws of England,* written almost two centuries after *Romeo and Juliet,* contains a discussion of "assaults committed by masters and mistresses on apprentice and servants . . . , so as to endanger life, or permanently injure health." Parents in Renaissance times had absolute rights over their children, and "there were similarities between the position of servants in the household and that of children in the family. . . . Both owed obedience and service to the head of the household." It is generally speaking true that the sixteenth century saw "the ultimately successful assertion of a royal monopoly of violence both public and private." But it is also true that "In the sixteenth and seventeenth century tempers were short and weapons to hand. . . . [A] gentleman carried a weapon at all times, and did not hesitate to use it. It was none other than Philip Sidney who warned his father's secretary that if he read his letters to his father again "I will thrust my dagger into you. And trust to it, for I speak it in earnest."[8]

Lord Herbert of Cherbury, himself a good poet and the older brother of a great one, George Herbert, writes unashamedly in his autobiography that, in January 1609, a ship on which he was returning from France began to break apart. A boat, a "shalop," set off from Dover: "I got into it first with my sword in my hand, and called for Sir Thomas Lucy [the only other man of rank on board], saying that if any man offer'd to get in before him, I should resist him with my sword . . . [A]fter I had receiv'd [Lucy], [I] bid the Shalop make away to shoar."[9]

Rapiers, dueling, sword masters, and sword-fighting treatises were usually Italian imports, as Shakespeare of course well knew. It was all something of an Elizabethan craze. And as A. L. Rowse notes, it is socially significant "that the duel now vindicated, not loyalty or the law, but 'personal honour, pride, or vanity.'"[10] Even the dinner table could be a source of serious violence, for it was a sobering fact needing to be reckoned with that literally everyone ate by impaling food on knives, usually sharp ones that diners brought to the table themselves. Forks, which were the replacement for knives, were an Italian invention that did not come into use, in England, until 1611.[11]

Violence-loving aristocrats, from the sober and imperious Duke to the dancers at Capulet's festive ball, are plainly at the center of *Romeo and Juliet*. But as he so often does, Shakespeare brings onto his stage a good many representatives of Renaissance England's lower classes, and not simply as traditionally "low," or comic, characters. Even Sampson and Gregory, two of the "heartless hinds" at whom Tybalt sneers (1.1.75), are a good deal more than mere buffoons. All Elizabethans relished quick wits and nimble tongues; these two members of the serving classes demonstrate both—and their punning jests quickly turn, as male prattle has always done, to matters bawdy. "I will take the wall of any man or maid of Montague's," says Sampson, adding that "women, being the weaker vessels, are ever thrust to the wall" (1.1.24–25, 28–29). And in the broader senses of the phrase, these two keep their wits about them: "Fear me not," says Sampson, assuring Gregory of his support. And Gregory, knowing his companion only too well, at once replies, "No, marry," as far as your support goes, "I fear thee!" (lines 47–48). The nameless and illiterate servant sent as a messenger, bearing invitations to a written list of persons, shows more good sense than Capulet, who dispatches him (and to whose order any lowbred protest would plainly be risky): "Find them out whose names are written here? It is written that the shoemaker should meddle with his yard and the tailor with his last, the fisher with his pencil and the painter with his nets, but I am sent to find those persons whose names are here writ, and can never find what names the writing person hath here writ" (1.2.38–42).

Still, it is only Juliet's Nurse, among the play's servants, whose role assumes major proportions. Having spent all fourteen of Juliet's years in relatively intimate association with the Capulet family, she has taken on a status poised somewhere between aristocratic and plebian. It is the Nurse to whom Lady Capulet hands the keys to locked store rooms—keys necessarily denied to mere servants, since locking such doors is expressly intended, and perfectly understood by everyone, to keep servants from stealing (4.4.1). It is the Nurse who is admitted to Lady Capulet's "counsel" with her daughter (1.3.9); the Nurse who, told by Lady Capulet to "hold thy peace," continues to ramble on (line 49); the Nurse who has the temerity, not only to scold her master for his usage of Juliet, but to protest his demeaning reply: "I speak no treason. . . . May one not speak?" (3.5.172, 173). And perhaps most impressively, it is the Nurse who participates essentially as an equal in the quasi-choral dirge spoken for Juliet by Capulet, Lady Capulet, and Paris (4.5.22–64).

Romeo and Juliet was, in the words of our time, a smash hit. "All the young men quoted it," observes Muriel Bradbrook.[12] It has remained a smash hit: no one, I think, has explained that fact so well as Mark Van Doren: "Few other plays, even by Shakespeare, engage the audience so intimately. . . . The tension of the entire

play, while we await the kiss of fire and powder which will con-
sume its most precious persons, is maintained at an endurable
point by the simplicity with which sorrow is made lyric. Even the
conceits ['metaphors'] of Romeo and Juliet sound like things that
they and they alone would say. . . . [W]ith a correct and powerful
understanding of the surrendered heart, the listening mind . . .
[Shakespeare] spares nothing yet handles gently."[13]

The purpose of this book is to make *Romeo and Juliet*'s glowing
words as readily accessible as if they had just been written.

Notes

1. David Cressy, *Birth, Marriage and Death: Ritual, Religion, and the Life-Cycle in Tudor and Stuart England* (Oxford: Oxford University Press, 1997), 311.

2. Will Durant, *The Renaissance* (New York: Simon and Schuster, 1953), 578.

3. Lawrence Stone, *The Family, Sex and Marriage in England, 1500–1800* (New York: Harper, 1977), 87.

4. Rosalie L. Colie, *Shakespeare's Living Art* (Princeton, N.J.: Princeton University Press, 1974), 23.

5. Lawrence Stone, *The Crisis of the Aristocracy, 1558–1641,* abridged ed. (Oxford: Oxford University Press, 1967), 20, 18.

6. "London's Vagrant Economy," in *Material London, ca. 1600,* ed. Lena Cowan Orlin (Philadelphia: University of Pennsylvania Press, 2000), 211.

7. Alexander Cowan, *Urban Europe, 1500–1700* (London: Hodder, 1998), 71–72.

8. Stone, *Crisis of the Aristocracy,* 20, 18, 97, 108.

9. *The Life of Edward, First Lord Herbert of Cherbury, Written by Himself,* ed. J. M. Shuttleworth (Oxford: Oxford University Press, 1976), 51.

10. A. L. Rowse, *The Elizabethan Renaissance: The Life of the Society* (London: Macmillan, 1971), 197.

11. Margaret Visser, *The Rituals of Dinner* (New York: Grove Weidenfeld, 1991), 186, 190.
12. Muriel Bradbrook, *Shakespeare: The Poet in His World* (New York: Columbia University Press, 1978), 99.
13. Mark Van Doren, *Shakespeare* (New York: Holt, 1939), 59–60.

SOME ESSENTIALS OF THE
SHAKESPEAREAN STAGE

The Stage

- There was no *scenery* (backdrops, flats, and so on).

- Compared to today's elaborate, high-tech productions, the Elizabethan stage had few *on-stage* props. These were mostly handheld: a sword or dagger, a torch or candle, a cup or flask. Larger props, such as furniture, were used sparingly.

- Costumes (some of which were upper-class castoffs, belonging to the individual actors) were elaborate. As in most premodern and very hierarchical societies, clothing was the distinctive mark of who and what a person was.

- What the actors *spoke,* accordingly, contained both the dramatic and narrative material we have come to expect in a theater (or movie house) and (1) the setting, including details of the time of day, the weather, and so on, and (2) the occasion. The *dramaturgy* is thus very different from that of our own time, requiring much more attention to verbal and gestural matters. Strict realism was neither intended nor, under the circumstances, possible.

- There was *no curtain*. Actors entered and left via doors in the back of the stage, behind which was the "tiring-room," where actors put on or changed their costumes.

- In *public theaters* (which were open-air structures), there was no *lighting;* performances could take place only in daylight hours.

- For *private* theaters, located in large halls of aristocratic houses, candlelight illumination was possible.

The Actors

- Actors worked in *professional* for-profit companies, sometimes organized and owned by other actors, and sometimes by entrepreneurs who could afford to erect or rent the company's building. Public theaters could hold, on average, two thousand playgoers, most of whom viewed and listened while standing. Significant profits could be and were made. Private theaters were smaller, more exclusive.

- There was *no director.* A book-holder / prompter / props manager, standing in the tiring-room behind the backstage doors, worked from a text marked with entrances and exits and notations of any special effects required for that particular script. A few such books have survived. Actors had texts only of their own parts, speeches being cued to a few prior words. There were few and often no rehearsals, in our modern use of the term, though there was often some coaching of individuals. Since Shakespeare's England was largely an oral culture, actors learned their parts rapidly and retained them for years. This was *repertory* theater, repeating popular plays and introducing some new ones each season.

- *Women* were not permitted on the professional stage. Most
  female roles were acted by *boys;* elderly women were played
  by grown men.

The Audience

- London's professional theater operated in what might be
  called a "red-light" district, featuring brothels, restaurants, and
  the kind of *open-air entertainment* then most popular, like bear-
  baiting (in which a bear, tied to a stake, was set on by dogs).

- A theater audience, like most of the population of Shakespeare's
  England, was largely made up of *illiterates.* Being able to read
  and write, however, had nothing to do with intelligence or
  concern with language, narrative, and characterization. People
  attracted to the theater tended to be both extremely verbal and
  extremely volatile. Actors were sometimes attacked, when the
  audience was dissatisfied; quarrels and fights were relatively
  common. Women were regularly in attendance, though no
  reliable statistics exist.

- Drama did not have the cultural esteem it has in our time,
  and plays were not regularly printed. Shakespeare's often
  appeared in book form, but not with any supervision or other
  involvement on his part. He wrote a good deal of nondramatic
  poetry as well, yet so far as we know he did not authorize or
  supervise *any* work of his that appeared in print during his
  lifetime.

- Playgoers, who had paid good money to see and hear, plainly
  gave dramatic performances careful, detailed attention. For some
  closer examination of such matters, see Burton Raffel, "Who

Heard the Rhymes and How: Shakespeare's Dramaturgical Signals," *Oral Tradition* 11 (October 1996): 190–221, and Raffel, "Metrical Dramaturgy in Shakespeare's Earlier Plays," *CEA Critic* 57 (Spring–Summer 1995): 51–65.

Romeo and Juliet

CHARACTERS (DRAMATIS PERSONAE)

Chorus
Escalus (Prince of Verona)
Paris (a young Count, the Prince's kinsman)
Montague and *Capulet* (heads of two feuding families)
An older, unnamed Capulet
Romeo (Montague's son)
Tybalt (Lady Capulet's nephew)
Mercutio (the Prince's kinsman and Romeo's friend)
Benvolio (Montague's nephew and Romeo's friend)
Friar Laurence (a Franciscan monk)
Friar John (a Franciscan monk)
Balthasar (Romeo's servant)
Abram (Montague's servant)
Sampson (Capulet's servant)
Gregory (Capulet's servant)
Peter (servant of Juliet's Nurse)
An Apothecary
Three Musicians
Three Watchmen
An Officer
Lady Montague (Montague's wife)
Lady Capulet (Capulet's wife)
Juliet (Capulet's daughter)
Juliet's Nurse
Citizens of Verona, Gentlemen and *Gentlewomen* of both houses,
    Maskers,[1] *Torchbearers, Pages, Guards, Servants,* and *Attendants*

1 persons disguised by a mask

Act I

ENTER Chorus[1]

Chorus Two households, both alike in dignity,[2]
In fair[3] Verona, where we lay our scene,[4]
From ancient grudge[5] break to new mutiny,[6]
Where civil[7] blood makes civil[8] hands unclean.[9]
From forth[10] the fatal[11] loins of these two foes[12]   5
A pair of star-crossed[13] lovers take[14] their life,

1 a single actor, representing/speaking for the entire troupe of actors
2 rank, nobleness, merit
3 beautiful, pleasing, delightful★
4 lay our scene = place/set our play
5 ill will
6 break to new mutiny = burst into new discord/quarrel
7 communal
8 (1) communal, (2) becoming, proper, decent
9 impure, foul
10 from forth = out of
11 fated, doomed
12 the Capulets and the Montagues
13 star-crossed = subject to malignant astrological influence
14 receive, obtain

Whose misadventured[15] piteous overthrows[16]
Doth with their death bury[17] their parents' strife.
The fearful[18] passage[19] of their death-marked love,
10 And the continuance of their parents' rage,
Which, but[20] their children's end, naught[21] could remove,
Is now the two hours' traffic[22] of our stage,
    The which if you with patient ears attend,[23]
    What here shall miss,[24] our toil shall strive to mend.

EXIT

SCENE I
Verona. A public place

ENTER SAMPSON AND GREGORY, BOTH CAPULETS

15 *Sampson* Gregory, on my word, we'll not carry[25] coals.[26]
Gregory No, for then we should be colliers.[27]
Sampson I mean, an[28] we be in choler, we'll draw.[29]

---

15 unfortunate
16 ruin, destruction (noun)
17 (1) inter, (2) abandon
18 dreadful, terrible, awful★
19 movement, course, progression, path
20 except for
21 nothing★
22 business
23 listen, consider, follow closely★
24 be lacking
25 submit to
26 insults (thrown like lumps of coals)
27 (1) dealers in / transporters of coal, (2) angry, wrathful ("choler"), (3) wearing
    dog- or prison-collars, and (4) the hangman's noose (neck collar)
28 if★
29 pull a sword from its sheath★

Gregory Ay, while you live, draw your neck out of collar.

Sampson I strike quickly, being moved.[30]

Gregory But thou art not quickly moved to strike.   20

Sampson A dog[31] of the house[32] of Montague moves me.

Gregory To move is to stir, and to be valiant is to stand.[33]
    Therefore, if thou art moved, thou runn'st away.

Sampson A dog of that house shall move me to stand. I will take
    the wall[34] of any man or maid of Montague's.   25

Gregory That shows thee a weak slave,[35] for the weakest goes
    to the wall.[36]

Sampson 'Tis true, and therefore women, being the weaker
    vessels,[37] are ever[38] thrust to the wall.[39] Therefore I will push
    Montague's men from the wall and thrust his maids[40] to the   30
    wall.

Gregory The quarrel is between our masters and us their men.

Sampson 'Tis all one. I will show myself a tyrant. When I have
    fought with the men, I will be civil[41] with the maids: I will
    cut off their heads.   35

Gregory The heads of the maids?

Sampson Ay, the heads of the maids, or their maidenheads.[42]

---

30 provoked, stirred up, angered★
31 a dog = a worthless/despicable person, coward
32 household
33 (1) remain firm/steadfast, (2) have an erection
34 take the wall = keep one's place on the inner side of a walkway/pavement
35 rascal, fellow★ (always negative)
36 succumbs, is defeated
37 weaker vessels = having less strength/capacity than men
38 always★
39 thrust to the wall = (1) defeated, (2) copulated with, against a wall
40 (1) women servants, (2) virgins
41 kind, courteous
42 virginity (the hymen/virginal membrane)

Take it in what sense[43] thou wilt.

Gregory They must take it in sense that feel it.

40 *Sampson* Me they shall feel, while I am able to stand[44] – and 'tis known I am a pretty piece of flesh.[45]

Gregory 'Tis well thou art not fish. If thou hadst,[46] thou hadst been poor John.[47] Draw thy tool![48] Here comes two of the house of Montagues.[49]

ENTER TWO OTHER SERVINGMEN, ABRAM AND BALTHASAR

45 *Sampson* My naked weapon is out.[50] Quarrel! I will back thee.

Gregory How? Turn thy back[51] and run?

Sampson Fear me not.[52]

Gregory No, marry.[53] I fear thee![54]

Sampson Let us take[55] the law of our sides.[56] Let them begin.

50 *Gregory* I will frown as I pass by, and let them take it as they list.[57]

---

43 in what sense = what (1) meaning, (2) physical feeling (of the five senses)
44 remain (1) on my feet , (2) with penis erect
45 pretty piece of flesh = (1) handsome, well-made man, (2) sexually well endowed/of considerable genital size
46 were
47 poor John = dried salt cod, a poor man's food
48 (1) weapon of war, (2) penis
49 (singular and plural, in Elizabethan English, are often used differently from modern usage)
50 (more sexual punning)
51 turn thy back: deliberately provoking misunderstanding of "back you"
52 fear me not = don't worry about me
53 exclamatory: oh yes!★
54 I fear thee = I'm afraid of you (being behind me? being disloyal?)
55 (1) follow, affirm, be careful to keep, make use of (2) act as if
56 of our sides = on our side
57 please (verb)

Sampson Nay, as they dare.[58] I will bite my thumb[59] at them, which is disgrace to them, if they bear it.

Abram Do you bite your thumb at us, sir?

Sampson I do bite my thumb, sir.   55

Abram Do you bite your thumb at us, sir?

Sampson (*aside to Gregory*) Is the law of[60] our side if I say ay?

Gregory (*aside to Sampson*) No.

Sampson No, sir, I do not bite my thumb at you, sir. But I bite my thumb, sir.   60

Gregory Do you quarrel, sir?

Abram Quarrel, sir? No, sir.

Sampson But if you do, sir, I am for you.[61] I serve as good a man as you.

Abram No better.   65

Sampson Well, sir.[62]

ENTER BENVOLIO[63]

Gregory (*aside to Sampson*) Say "better." Here comes one of my master's kinsmen.

Sampson Yes, better, sir.

Abram You lie.   70

Sampson Draw, if you be[64] men. Gregory, remember thy

---

58 have the courage/boldness
59 bite my thumb = snap my thumb nail with my upper teeth (derisive, condescending)
60 on
61 I am for you = I am ready/a match for you
62 (equivocal remark, indicating uncertainty, indecision)
63 (benVOLyo)
64 are (subjunctive)

swashing[65] blow.

Benvolio (*beating down their swords*) Part fools!
　　Put up[66] your swords. You know not what you do.

75　*Tybalt*　What, art thou drawn[67] among these heartless hinds?[68]
　　Turn thee, Benvolio! Look upon thy death.
　　Benvolio　I do but[69] keep the peace. Put up thy sword,
　　Or manage[70] it to part[71] these men with[72] me.
　　Tybalt　What, drawn, and talk of peace? I hate the word
80　As I hate hell, all Montagues, and thee.
　　Have at thee,[73] coward!

Officer　Clubs, bills,[75] and partisans! Strike! Beat them down!
Citizens　Down with the Capulets! Down with the Montagues!

65 slashing
66 away
67 with your sword out
68 drawn among these heartless hinds = wielding your sword among such
　spiritless/foolish domestic servants
69 but = only★
70 wield, use
71 separate
72 along with
73 have at thee = (an imperative, announcing an attack)
74 long-handled spears with various lateral cutting projections
75 long-handled, sometimes concave axe-like weapons with spikes jutting in
　the other direction from their blades

ENTER CAPULET IN HIS GOWN,[76] AND LADY CAPULET

Capulet	What noise is this? Give me my long sword,[77] ho!
Lady Capulet	A crutch, a crutch! Why call you for a sword? 85
Capulet	My sword, I say! Old Montague is come.

And flourishes[78] his blade in spite of [79] me.

ENTER MONTAGUE AND LADY MONTAGUE

Montague	Thou villain[80] Capulet! – (*to Lady Montague*)

Hold me not, let me go.

Lady Montague Thou shalt not stir one foot to seek a foe.

ENTER PRINCE, WITH HIS ATTENDANTS

Prince	Rebellious subjects, enemies to peace, 90

Profaners[81] of this neighbor-stainèd steel:[82]
Will they not hear? What, ho! You men, you beasts,[83]
That quench the fire of your pernicious[84] rage
With purple fountains issuing from your veins:
On pain of torture, from those bloody hands   95
Throw your mistempered[85] weapons to the ground

---

76 nightgown, dressing gown, bathrobe
77 long sword = sword with long cutting blade
78 brandishes, waves about
79 in spite of = as an insult to/in hatred/contempt for
80 (1) lowborn peasant, (2) rascal, scoundrel★
81 defilers, violators
82 neighbor-stainèd steel = weapons stained with the blood of your neighbors
83 men of animal nature
84 destructive, ruinous, fatal
85 (1) tempered for evil purpose, (2) disorderly (steel is "tempered" in its manufacture)

And hear the sentence[86] of your movèd[87] prince.

Three civil[88] brawls, bred of[89] an airy[90] word

By thee, old Capulet, and Montague,

100 Have thrice disturbed the quiet of our streets

And made Verona's ancient[91] citizens

Cast by[92] their grave,[93] beseeming ornaments[94]

To wield old partisans, in hands as[95] old,

Cankered[96] with peace, to part[97] your cankered[98] hate.

105 If ever you disturb our streets again

Your lives shall pay[99] the forfeit[100] of the peace.

For this time[101] all the rest depart away.

You, Capulet, shall[102] go along with me,

And, Montague, come you this afternoon,

110 To know our[103] farther pleasure[104] in this case,[105]

86 authoritative decision/judgment
87 indignant, angered
88 civil = community wide/among citizens
89 bred of = generated by/born of
90 (1) lightly spoken, flippant (2) empty, imaginary
91 aged, old, venerable
92 cast by = throw away/aside, shed, drop
93 respected, revered
94 beseeming ornaments = appropriate/befitting* equipment/accessories
95 just as, equally
96 rusted, corroded
97 break up
98 infected, gangrened, depraved
99 pay for
100 breach, violation
101 this time = now
102 must
103 the royal "we," meaning "I"
104 farther pleasure = additional wishes
105 set of circumstances

To old Freetown, our common judgment place.[106]
Once more, on pain[107] of death, all men depart.[108]

EXEUNT ALL BUT[109] MONTAGUE, LADY MONTAGUE,
AND BENVOLIO

Montague Who set this ancient quarrel new abroach[110]?
  Speak, nephew. Were you by[111] when it began?
Benvolio   Here were the servants of your adversary   115
  And yours, close fighting[112] ere[113] I did approach.
  I drew to part them. In the instant[114] came
  The fiery Tybalt, with his sword prepared,[115]
  Which as[116] he breathed defiance[117] to my ears,
  He swung about[118] his head and cut the winds,   120
  Who, nothing hurt withal,[119] hissed him in scorn.
  While we were interchanging thrusts and blows,
  Came more and more, and fought on part and part,[120]
  Till the Prince came, who parted either part.[121]

---

106 common judgment place = general/usual decision-making place
107 penalty, punishment
108 go away (a command)
109 except
110 set . . . abroach = set astir, afoot (set abroach a cask/barrel of liquor = to
     open)
111 in the vicinity, close by
112 close fighting = fighting hard/at close quarters
113 before★
114 in the instant = at that moment
115 at the ready, drawn from its sheath
116 even as
117 breathed defiance = exhaled/spoke hostility/challenge
118 around★
119 therewith
120 on part and part = some on one side and some on the other
121 parted either part = separated each side/both sides

125   *Lady Montague*   O, where is Romeo? Saw you him to-day?

          Right glad I am he was not at this fray.

      Benvolio   Madam, an hour before the worshipped[122] sun

          Peered forth[123] the golden window of the East,

          A troubled mind drove me to walk abroad,[124]

130   Where underneath the grove of sycamore

          That westward rooteth[125] from the city's side[126]

          So early walking did I see your son.

          Towards him I made,[127] but he was ware[128] of me

          And stole[129] into the covert[130] of the wood.

135   I – measuring[131] his affections[132] by my own,

          Which then most sought where most[133] might not be found,

          Being one too many by[134] my weary[135] self –

          Pursued[136] my humor,[137] not pursuing his,

          And gladly shunned who[138] gladly fled from me.

140   *Montague*   Many a morning hath he there been seen,

          With tears augmenting the fresh morning's dew,

122 adored, venerated
123 forth from
124 in the open air
125 grows
126 outskirts
127 went, headed
128 wary
129 quietly withdrew★
130 shelter, dense / thickly grown part
131 judging, evaluating
132 feelings, emotions, state of mind★
133 most sought where most = principally sought where most people
134 all by
135 (1) discontented, dispirited, depressed, (2) tiresome
136 followed
137 mood★
138 he who

Adding to clouds more clouds with his deep sighs,
But all so soon as the all-cheering sun
Should in the farthest East begin to draw
The shady curtains[139] from Aurora's[140] bed,   145
Away from light steals home my heavy[141] son
And private in his chamber pens himself,
Shuts up his windows, locks fair[142] daylight out
And makes himself an artificial night.
Black[143] and portentous[144] must this humor prove,[145]   150
Unless good counsel[146] may the cause remove.

Benvolio   My noble uncle, do you know the cause?

Montague   I neither know it nor can learn of[147] him.

Benvolio   Have you importuned[148] him by any means?[149]

Montague   Both by myself and many other friends.   155
But he, his own affections' counselor,
Is to himself — I will not say how true —
But to himself so secret and so close,[150]
So far from sounding and discovery,[151]

---

139 (bed curtains were in common use)
140 the dawn
141 (1) grave, severe, somber, (2) troubled, sad, despondent
142 fine
143 melancholy, dismal
144 ominous, threatening
145 demonstrate/turn out to be
146 advice, guidance, judgment★
147 from
148 urged, pressed
149 by any means = in any way★
150 uncommunicative
151 sounding and discovery = investigation/determination and explanation/
   disclosure

160 As is the bud bit with[152] an envious[153] worm
Ere he can spread his sweet leaves to the air
Or dedicate[154] his beauty to the sun.
Could we but learn from whence his sorrows grow
We would as willingly give cure as[155] know.

ENTER ROMEO

165 *Benvolio*   See, where he comes. So please you step aside,
I'll know his grievance,[156] or be much denied.[157]
Montague I would thou wert[158] so happy by thy stay[159]
To hear[160] true shrift.[161] Come, madam, let's away.

EXEUNT MONTAGUE AND LADY MONTAGUE

Benvolio   Good morrow,[162] cousin.[163]
Romeo   Is the day so young?
Benvolio   But new[164] struck nine.
170 *Romeo*   Ay me! sad hours seem long.
Was that my father that went hence so fast?
Benvolio   It was. What sadness lengthens Romeo's hours?

152 by
153 malicious, spiteful★
154 devote, open
155 as we would
156 the cause / nature of his grief
157 much denied = deeply / intensely refused / rejected
158 would thou wert = wish you might be
159 by thy stay = on account of your remaining here
160 to hear = that you will hear
161 true shrift = honest / sincere / reliable penance / repentance
162 morning, day★
163 relative, any member of the larger family (often shortened to "coz")★
164 newly, just

Romeo   Not having that which having[165] makes them short.

Benvolio In love?

Romeo   Out –   175

Benvolio Of love?

Romeo   Out of her favor,[166] where I am in love.

Benvolio Alas that love, so gentle[167] in his view,[168]

   Should be so tyrannous and rough[169] in proof.[170]

Romeo   Alas that love, whose view is muffled still,[171]   180

   Should without eyes[172] see pathways to his will.[173]

   Where shall we dine? (*looks around*) O me! What fray was
   here?

   Yet tell me not, for I have heard it all.

   Here's much to do with hate, but more with love.[174]

   Why then, O brawling love, O loving hate,   185

   O anything of[175] nothing first create![176]

   O heavy lightness, serious vanity![177]

   Misshapen chaos of well-seeming[178] forms!

165 if one has it
166 good graces
167 courteous, noble★
168 in his view = in his ("its") appearance
169 disagreeable, harsh★
170 in proof = how it turns out / is experienced
171 view is muffled still = whose sight is forever / always blinded
172 without eyes: Cupid is blind
173 pleasure, desire
174 (if "here" = the setting / location, because Rosaline, his current love, is a
     Capulet [and thus with "hate"]; if "here" = inside Romeo, because his
     heart is all awhirl)
175 from, out of
176 created
177 futility, foolishness, idleness
178 appearing★ to be good

Feather of lead, bright smoke, cold fire, sick health,
190 Still[179] waking sleep, that is not what it is!
This love feel I, that feel no love[180] in this.
Dost thou not laugh?

Benvolio   No, coz, I rather weep.

Romeo Good heart,[181] at what?

Benvolio   At thy good heart's
oppression.[182]

Romeo Why, such is love's transgression.[183]
195 Griefs of mine own lie heavy in my breast,
Which[184] thou wilt propagate,[185] to have it pressed[186]
With more of thine.[187] This love that thou hast shown
Doth add more grief to too much of mine own.[188]
Love is a smoke raised[189] with the fume[190] of sighs;
200 Being purged,[191] a fire sparkling in lovers' eyes;
Being vexed,[192] a sea nourished with lovers' tears.
What is it else?[193] A madness most discreet,[194]

179 (adverb)
180 feel no love = take no pleasure
181 (used like *mon ami,* in French)
182 burden, grief, trouble
183 sin
184 which griefs
185 multiply
186 have it pressed = squeeze my heart
187 your love for me
188 too much of mine own = my own grief, already too much
189 caused, roused, provoked
190 with the fume = by the exhalation/vapors
191 washed away, purified
192 irritated, annoyed, grieved
193 besides, in addition*
194 (1) cautious, judicious, prudent, (2) courteous, polite

A choking gall,[195] and a preserving sweet.[196]

Farewell, my coz.

Benvolio   Soft![197] I will go along.[198]

An[199] if you leave me so, you do me wrong.   205

Romeo   Tut! I have lost myself, I am not here.

This is not Romeo, he's some other where.

Benvolio Tell me in sadness,[200] who is that you love?

Romeo   What, shall I groan and tell thee?

Benvolio   Groan? Why, no.

But sadly tell me who.   210

Romeo   Bid[201] a sick man in sadness make his will.

Ah, word ill[202] urged to one that is so ill.

In sadness, cousin, I do love a woman.

Benvolio I aimed so near[203] when I supposed you loved.

Romeo   A right good markman,[204] and she's fair[205] I love.   215

Benvolio A right fair[206] mark,[207] fair[208] coz, is soonest hit.

Romeo   Well, in that hit[209] you miss. She'll not be hit

195 choking gall = smothering bitterness
196 preserving sweet = preservative sweetness
197 wait a minute!
198 along with you
199 and
200 in sadness = in earnest
201 ask, entreat, beg
202 harshly, hurtfully, wrongfully, blamefully
203 closely
204 marksman
205 beautiful
206 right fair = proper/upright fine/pleasing
207 target
208 (term of respect/courtesy: Shakespeare uses "fair" three ways in the space of eight words)
209 stroke, guess

With Cupid's arrow. She hath Dian's[210] wit,[211]

And, in strong proof of chastity well armed,[212]

220 From Love's[213] weak childish bow she lives unharmed.

She will not stay[214] the siege of loving terms,[215]

Nor bide[216] th' encounter[217] of assailing[218] eyes,

Nor ope[219] her lap[220] to saint-seducing gold.

O she's rich in beauty, only poor

225 That, when she dies, with beauty dies her store.[221]

Benvolio Then she hath sworn that she will still live chaste?

Romeo   She hath, and in that sparing[222] makes huge waste,

For beauty, starved with her[223] severity,[224]

Cuts beauty off from all posterity.

230 She is too fair, too wise, wisely too fair,

To merit bliss[225] by making me despair.

She hath forsworn[226] to Love, and in that vow

Do I live dead that live to tell it now.

210 Diana = goddess of hunting and of chastity
211 mental capacity, intellectual power (also "wits")★
212 equipped for battle
213 Cupid's
214 quietly endure ("sustain, abide by, depend on, support")
215 (1) conditions, (2) words
216 submit to, tolerate
217 face-to-face meeting, skirmish, duel
218 attacking, assaulting
219 open
220 (1) front of a skirt, (2) female genitalia
221 with beauty dies her store = what dies, along with her beauty, is her
    capacity for reproduction
222 saving, frugality, economy
223 Rosaline's
224 strictness, sternness, moral austerity
225 merit bliss = deserve/obtain her (Rosaline's) (1) happiness, (2) salvation
226 falsely sworn, perjured herself

Benvolio Be ruled[227] by me: forget to think of her.

Romeo O teach me how I should forget to think.   235

Benvolio By giving liberty unto thine eyes.

    Examine other beauties.

Romeo   'Tis the way

    To call hers – exquisite – in question[228] more.

    These happy[229] masks that kiss fair ladies' brows,

    Being black[230] puts us in mind they hide the fair.   240

    He that is stricken blind cannot forget

    The precious treasure of his eyesight lost.

    Show me a mistress[231] that is passing[232] fair,

    What doth her beauty serve but as a note[233]

    Where I may read[234] who passed[235] that passing fair?   245

    Farewell. Thou canst not teach me to forget.

Benvolio I'll pay[236] that doctrine,[237] or else die in debt.[238]

EXEUNT

227 guided★
228 call hers – exquisite – in question more = call/summon even more to
    mind her beauty, which is exquisite
229 lucky, fortunate
230 (1) black (color), (2) unattractive
231 woman commanding a man's heart, lady love
232 surpassing, transcendentally★
233 sign, token
234 see, find
235 surpassed
236 discharge the obligation of
237 lesson, knowledge
238 die in debt = die trying

SCENE 2
A street

ENTER CAPULET, COUNT PARIS, AND HIS SERVANT

Capulet But Montague is bound[1] as well as I,
    In penalty alike, and 'tis not hard, I think,
    For men so old as we to keep the peace.

Paris   Of honorable reckoning[2] are you both,
5   And pity 'tis you lived at odds so long.
    But now, my lord, what say you to my suit?[3]

Capulet But saying o'er what I have said before.
    My child is yet a stranger[4] in the world:
    She hath not seen the change[5] of fourteen years.
10   Let two more summers wither[6] in their pride
    Ere we may think her ripe to be a bride.

Paris   Younger than she are happy mothers made.

Capulet And too soon marred[7] are those so early made.
    The earth hath swallowed all my hopes[8] but she:
15   She is the hopeful[9] lady of my earth.[10]
    But woo her, gentle Paris, get her heart.
    My will to her consent is but a part.

1 (1) constrained, compelled, (2) under bond?
2 account, distinction
3 (1) supplication, request, (2) wooing, courting (paternal approval being primary)
4 newcomer
5 changing, succession, passing
6 shrivel, fade away
7 spoiled, injured, disfigured
8 expectations: children
9 full of/laden with hope
10 my earth = my life (and hopes)

An she agree, within[11] her scope[12] of choice
Lies my consent and fair according[13] voice.
This night I hold an old accustomed feast[14]   20
Whereto[15] I have invited many a guest,
Such as I love – and you among[16] the store,[17]
One more, most welcome, makes my number[18] more.
At my poor house look[19] to behold this night
Earth-treading[20] stars that make dark heaven light.[21]   25
Such comfort[22] as do lusty[23] young men feel
When well appareled[24] April on the heel
Of limping[25] Winter treads, even such delight
Among fresh fennel[26] buds shall you this night
Inherit[27] at my house. Hear all, all see,   30
And like her most whose merit most shall be,
Which, on more view of many, mine,[28] being one,
May stand in number,[29] though in reck'ning none.[30]

11 inside, in the limits of, contained within
12 sphere, range, freedom
13 agreeing, matching, harmonious
14 accustomed feast = customary/habitual gathering/entertainment/banquet★
15 to which
16 you among = to add you to
17 company, abundance of persons
18 my number = the count of my guests
19 expect
20 walking, stepping, dancing
21 make dark heaven light = light up the dark sky
22 refreshment, invigoration, pleasure, delight
23 lively, merry, joyful
24 clothed, adorned (winter being bare, and April marking the coming of spring)
25 lame (by April, winter is old and enfeebled, ready to die)
26 savory herb with yellow flowers (some texts have "female")
27 receive, take possession of
28 my daughter (Juliet)
29 stand in number = stand out/be first/number one among them?
30 though in reck'ning none = though in the mathematics of probability one is
   not strictly speaking a number

Come, go with me.[31]

(*to Servant, giving him a paper*)

Go, sirrah,[32] trudge[33] about[34]

35 Through fair Verona. Find those persons out

Whose names are written there, and to them say

My house and welcome on their pleasure stay.[35]

EXEUNT CAPULET AND PARIS

Servant Find them out whose names are written here? It is

written that the shoemaker should meddle[36] with his yard[37]

40 and the tailor with his last,[38] the fisher with his pencil and the

painter with his nets. But I am sent to find those persons

whose names are here writ, and can never find[39] what names

the writing person hath here writ. I must to[40] the learnèd. In

good time!

ENTER BENVOLIO AND ROMEO

45 *Benvolio* Tut, man, one fire burns out another's burning,

One pain is lessened by another's[41] anguish.

31 come GO with ME (the first two feet of an iambic pentameter line)

32 (used for low-ranking men and boys instead of "sir," indicating authority or rebuke)★

33 (undignified word for "walking")

34 go SIRrah TRUDGE aBOUT (the last three feet of the same iambic pentameter line: a spatial break is not necessarily a metrical break)

35 tarry, await★

36 be concerned, busy himself with

37 yardstick (measuring rod – which a shoemaker of course does not use: the servant's "confusion" seems deliberate, intended by him to emphasize the foolishness of sending an illiterate on such an errand)

38 wooden model of the foot

39 discover, learn

40 must to = must go to

41 another pain's

Turn giddy,[42] and be holp[43] by backward turning.[44]

One desperate[45] grief cures with another's languish.[46]

Take thou some new infection to thy eye,[47]

And the rank[48] poison of the old will die.   50

Romeo   Your[49] plantain[50] leaf is excellent for that.

Benvolio   For what, I pray thee?

Romeo   For your broken[51] shin.

Benvolio   Why, Romeo, art thou mad?

Romeo   Not mad, but bound[52] more than a madman is,

Shut up in prison, kept without my food,   55

Whipped and tormented and – (*seeing Servant*) God den,[53]

good fellow.[54]

Servant   God gi' go den. I pray,[55] sir, can you read?

Romeo   Ay, mine own fortune[56] in my misery.

---

42 (1) light-headed, frivolous, (2) whirling in circles
43 helped
44 backward turning = facing the opposite way
45 dangerous, reckless, virtually hopeless★
46 sickness, decline, wasting away, suffering
47 (In *Rime Sparse*, 3.1304–74, foundation and source of Renaissance European
   love theory, Petrarch wrote of "the pathway from eyes to heart," along which
   the instantly irresistible force of love travels. One look and the lover has
   fallen; one mutual look, and love sweeps both lovers away.)
48 strong, violent, excessive
49 "the" rather than modern "your" (see Romeo's next speech for yet another
   such usage)
50 a low-growing herbal plant with broad, flat leaves, rather than the tropical
   tree with banana-like fruit
51 torn, bruised, wounded
52 fastened down, tied up
53 God den = good evening ("God give you good even")★
54 (customary form of address, in speaking to someone of humble station, a
   "common" person)
55 ask earnestly and politely
56 future

Servant Perhaps you have learned it without book.[57] But I pray,
60   can you read anything you see?

Romeo Ay, if I know the letters and the language.

Servant Ye say honestly.[58] Rest you merry![59]

Romeo Stay, fellow; I can read.

HE READS THE LETTER

"Signior Martino and his wife and daughters;
65   County Anselmo and his beauteous sisters;
The lady widow of Vitruvio;
Signior Placentio and his lovely nieces;
Mercutio and his brother Valentine;
Mine uncle Capulet, his wife and daughters;
70   My fair niece Rosaline, and Livia;
Signior Valentio and his cousin Tybalt;
Lucio and the lively Helena."

GIVES BACK THE PAPER

A fair[60] assembly. Whither should they come?

Servant Up.

75 *Romeo* Whither?

Servant To supper, to our house.

Romeo Whose house?

Servant My master's.

Romeo Indeed I should have asked you that before.

80 *Servant* Now I'll tell you without asking. My master is the great

57 without book = by heart
58 decently, worthily, without falseness
59 rest you merry = may you be merry/happy
60 fine, elegant

rich Capulet and if you be not of the house of Montagues,
I pray come and crush[61] a cup of wine. Rest you merry.

EXIT

Benvolio At this same ancient[62] feast of Capulet's
Sups the fair Rosaline whom thou so lov'st,
With all the admired beauties of Verona.   85
Go thither, and with unattainted[63] eye
Compare her face with some that I shall show,
And I will make thee think thy swan a crow.
Romeo When the devout religion of mine eye[64]
Maintains such falsehood, then[65] turn tears to fires,   90
And these[66] who, often drowned,[67] could never die,[68]
Transparent[69] heretics, be[70] burnt for liars.
One fairer than my love? The all-seeing sun
Ne'er[71] saw her match since first the world begun.
Benvolio Tut! You saw her fair, none else being by,   95
Herself poised with herself in either eye.[72]
But in that[73] crystal scales[74] let there be weighed

61 drink
62 ("old" in the sense of "traditional")
63 unspotted, free from blemish, clear
64 (see act 1, scene 2, note 47)
65 then let
66 those
67 in tears
68 (1) die (literally), (2) experience sexual orgasm
69 obvious
70 let them be
71 never*
72 herself poised with herself in either eye = Rosaline measured/balanced
   against herself in each of your two eyes
73 those
74 crystal scales = Romeo's eyes

Your lady's love[75] against some other maid

That I will show you shining at this feast,

100   And she[76] shall scant show[77] well that now seems best.

Romeo I'll go along,[78] no such sight to be shown,

But to rejoice in splendor of my own.[79]

EXEUNT

75 your lady's love = your love of this lady
76 the one (literally, the one "she")
77 scant show = hardly/barely seem/appear
78 go along = accompany you
79 splendor of my own = my own lady love's splendor

SCENE 3
Capulet's house

ENTER LADY CAPULET AND NURSE

Lady Capulet Nurse, where's my daughter? Call her forth[1] to
me.

Nurse Now, by my maidenhead at twelve year old,[2]
I bade[3] her come. What, lamb! what, ladybird![4]
God forbid. Where's this girl? What,[5] Juliet!

ENTER JULIET

Juliet How now?[6] Who calls?
Nurse Your mother.
Juliet Madam,
I'm here.   5
What is your will?
Lady Capulet This is the matter[7] – Nurse, give leave[8] awhile,
We must talk in secret. (*Nurse starts to leave*) Nurse, come back
again.
I have remembered me, thou's[9] hear our counsel.[10]
Thou knowest my daughter's of a pretty[11] age.   10

---

1 (1) out, (2) at once
2 (she can swear by it at twelve – but not thereafter)
3 urged, begged
4 sweetheart
5 well! / now! / hey!
6 how now = why
7 subject, theme, substance★
8 give leave = please leave
9 thou's = you are supposed to / must ("thou shalt")
10 consultation, exchange of opinions, conversation
11 fine, proper, pleasing

Nurse   Faith, I can tell her age unto an hour.

Lady Capulet She's not fourteen.

Nurse   I'll lay[12] fourteen of my teeth —

And yet, to my teen[13] be it spoken, I have but four —

She is not fourteen. How long is it now

To Lammastide?[14]

15   *Lady Capulet*   A fortnight[15] and odd[16] days.

Nurse   Even or odd,[17] of all days in the year,

Come Lammas Eve at night shall she be fourteen.

Susan[18] and she (God rest all Christian souls)

Were of an age. Well, Susan is with God,

20   She was too good for me. But as I said,

On Lammas Eve at night shall she be fourteen.[19]

That shall she. Marry, I remember it well.

'Tis since the earthquake now eleven years,

And she was weaned (I never shall forget it),

25   Of all the days of the year, upon that day,

For I had then laid wormwood to my dug,[20]

Sitting in the sun under the dovehouse[21] wall.

My lord and you were then at Mantua.

12 bet

13 sorrow, affliction

14 August 1 (harvest festival for early wheat crop: "Lammas wheat" = winter wheat))

15 two weeks ("fourteen" nights)

16 and odd = plus a few days over fourteen

17 (a pun on "odd" as just defined and "odd" as opposed to "even"?)

18 (the Nurse's dead daughter)

19 on LAMmas EVE at NIGHT shall SHE be fourTEEN (iambic pentameter is neither mechanical nor rigid)

20 laid wormwood to my dug = placed bitter herb on my nipple

21 pigeon house

Nay, I do bear[22] a brain. But as I said,

When it[23] did taste the wormwood on the nipple   30

Of my dug and felt it bitter,[24] pretty fool,[25]

To see it tetchy[26] and fall out[27] with the dug!

Shake,[28] quoth[29] the dovehouse![30] 'Twas no need, I trow,[31]

To bid me trudge.[32]

And since that time it is eleven years,   35

For then she could stand high lone.[33] Nay, by th' rood,[34]

She could have run and waddled[35] all about,

For even the day before she broke[36] her brow,[37]

And then my husband – God be with his soul,

'A[38] was a merry man – took up[39] the child.   40

"Yea," quoth he, "dost thou fall upon thy face?

Thou wilt fall backward[40] when thou hast more wit,

Wilt thou not, Jule?" and, by my holidam,[41]

22 (1) have, (2) still have (though old)
23 the baby
24 of my DUG and FELT it BITter
25 (term of endearment/pity, especially in speaking to/of children)
26 quickly irritable/annoyed
27 fall out = quarrel, disagree (verb)
28 get moving!
29 said
30 (the wall thereof shook, when the child started)
31 believe, expect, hope ("I can tell you")
32 go away, be off
33 high lone = alone, by herself
34 the cross on which Christ was crucified
35 swaying from one leg to the other, like a duck
36 cut
37 forehead
38 he★
39 took up = caught/lifted up
40 fall backward = have sexual intercourse
41 holy relic/place (variant spelling of "halidom," from Old English

The pretty wretch[42] left[43] crying, and said "Ay."
45   To see now how a jest shall come about.[44]
I warrant,[45] an I should live a thousand years,
I never should forget it. "Wilt thou not, Jule?" quoth he,
And, pretty fool,[46] it stinted[47] and said "Ay."

Lady Capulet   Enough of this. I pray thee hold thy peace.

50 *Nurse*   Yes, madam. Yet I cannot choose but laugh
To think it should leave crying and say "Ay."
And yet, I warrant, it had upon its brow
A bump as big as a young cock'rel's stone,[48]
A perilous knock,[49] and it cried bitterly.
55   "Yea," quoth my husband, "fall'st upon thy face?
Thou wilt fall backward when thou comest to age.[50]
Wilt thou not, Jule?" It stinted, and said "Ay."

Juliet   And stint thou too, I pray thee, Nurse, say I.

Nurse   Peace, I have done. God mark[51] thee to his grace,
60   Thou wast the prettiest babe that e'er I nursed.
An I might live to see thee married once,[52]
I have my wish.

"haligdom," meaning "sanctity/sanctuary": halig = holy, dom = custom,
power, glory)
42 pretty wretch = fine little person/creature
43 stopped
44 come about = come true
45 promise, pledge★
46 pretty fool = nice little innocent
47 stopped
48 young cock'rel's stone = (1) young cock's testicle, (2) young man's testicle
49 perilous knock = serious blow/thump
50 to age = old enough
51 God mark = may God set/make/identify
52 at some/any time

Lady Capulet Marry, that "marry" is the very[53] theme

    I came to talk of. Tell me, daughter Juliet,

    How stands your disposition[54] to be married?   65

Juliet   It is an honor that I dream not of.

Nurse   An honor? Were not I thine only nurse,

    I would say thou hadst sucked wisdom from thy teat.

Lady Capulet Well, think of marriage now.[55] Younger than you,

    Here in Verona, ladies of esteem,[56]   70

    Are made already mothers. By my count,

    I was your mother much upon[57] these years

    That you are now a maid.[58] Thus then in brief:[59]

    The valiant[60] Paris seeks you for his love.

Nurse   A man, young lady! Lady, such a man   75

    As all the world – why he's a man of wax.[61]

Lady Capulet Verona's summer hath not such a flower.

Nurse   Nay, he's a flower, in faith – a very[62] flower.

Lady Capulet What say you? Can you love the gentleman?

    This night you shall behold him at our feast.   80

    Read o'er the volume[63] of young Paris' face

    And find delight writ there with beauty's pen.

---

53 same, exact
54 bent of mind
55 think of marriage now = *now* think about marriage
56 ladies of esteem = reputable / well-respected ladies
57 much upon = approximately at
58 unmarried woman, virgin★
59 in brief = briefly, shortly, in a few words
60 (1) brave, courageous, (2) rich
61 man of wax = man of perfect figure / stature (a "model")
62 true, real★
63 book

Examine every married lineament[64]

And see how one another lends content[65] –

85   And what obscured[66] in this fair volume lies

Find written in the margent[67] of his eyes.

This precious book of love, this unbound[68] lover,

To beautify him only lacks a cover.[69]

The fish lives in the sea, and 'tis much pride

90   For fair without[70] the fair within to hide.[71]

That book[72] in many's eyes doth share the glory[73]

That in gold clasps[74] locks in the golden story.[75]

So shall you share all that he doth possess

By having him,[76] making yourself no less.[77]

95 *Nurse*   No less? Nay, bigger. Women grow by men.[78]

---

64 married lineament = joined/harmonious feature

65 one another lends content = one lends substance to another

66 hidden

67 comment written/printed in the margins

68 not tied up, (the pages) unrestrained/not secured

69 that which encloses (a book's cover), which shelters (body cover – armor, clothing), which supports (a wife!)

70 outside

71 the fish lives . . . to hide = just as the fish by its very nature lives in the sea, and shields/protects the fish that swim in it, so too it is a source of honest pride for one who is fair on the outside (a woman) to shield/protect one who is fair inside (a man)

72 the man

73 admiration, praise

74 gold clasps (noun) = gold fastenings (as costly books were then often so bound)

75 locks in the golden story = encloses/secures/confines the golden life ("story/history")

76 having him = (1) possessing him, (2) accepting him/his proposal of marriage ("will you have me?" spoken by a man to a woman, meant "will you marry me?")

77 no less = no less esteemed/worthy

78 (by being made pregnant)

Lady Capulet Speak briefly, can you like of[79] Paris' love?

Juliet I'll look to like,[80] if looking liking move,[81]

But no more deep will I endart[82] mine eye

Than your consent gives strength[83] to make it[84] fly.

ENTER SERVINGMAN

Servingman Madam, the guests are come, supper served up, 100
you called, my young lady asked for, the Nurse cursed in the
pantry,[85] and everything in extremity. I must hence to wait.
I beseech you follow straight.[86]

Lady Capulet We follow thee.

EXIT SERVINGMAN

Juliet, the County[87] stays.[88]

Nurse Go, girl, seek happy nights to[89] happy days. 105

EXEUNT

79 like of = approve, be pleased by
80 look to like = take care/be sure to consider/find out if I like (him/his
  proposal)
81 if looking liking move = if looking makes me want to like
82 pierce with my eye (the effect of which is discussed in act 1, scene 2, note 47:
  the usual meaning of "dart" is "arrow," which is Cupid's weapon)
83 power, force
84 (the antecedent of "it" is "mine eye," though the modern sense of "mine
  eye" is "my eyes")
85 storeroom for food and often for table linen and dishes (in the first line of act
  4, scene 4, the Nurse is given keys to the pantry; her absence therefrom is
  probably why she is being cursed)
86 directly, at once★ (though always printed as prose, this speech constitutes four
  iambic pentameter lines and contains two vivid internal rhymes, "nurse
  cursed" and "wait . . . straight.")
87 Count (equivalent of Earl)
88 waits
89 leading to? in addition to? accompanying, in accord with? connected to?

SCENE 4
A street

ENTER ROMEO, MERCUTIO, BENVOLIO, WITH FIVE OR SIX
OTHER MASKERS, AND TORCHBEARERS

Romeo   What, shall this speech be spoke[1] for our excuse?
  Or shall we on[2] without apology?
Benvolio The date is out of such prolixity.[3]
  We'll have no Cupid hoodwinked[4] with a scarf,[5]
5 Bearing a Tartar's[6] painted bow[7] of lath,[8]
  Scaring the ladies like a crowkeeper,[9]
  Nor no without book[10] prologue, faintly[11] spoke
  After the prompter,[12] for our entrance.[13]
  But let them measure[14] us by what they will,
10 We'll measure[15] them a measure,[16] and be gone.

1 speech . . . spoke (convention called for maskers, who were usually intruders, not invited/expected, to deliver a speech, flattering/propitiating the host and the invited guests)
2 proceed
3 the date is out of such prolixity = the custom of delivering a prolix speech is now out of date
4 blindfolded, and thus in effect blinded (as Cupid was often thought to be)
5 band, usually of silk
6 Central Asian
7 painted bow = something not a bow but painted to look like one
8 of lath = made of thin, narrow strips of wood
9 (1) scarecrow carrying a bow, (2) a field hand/boy hired to frighten crows
10 without book (adjectival) = memorized (as opposed to extemporaneous)
11 softly, hesitantly, uncertainly
12 after the prompter = following a prompter's reminders
13 for our entrance = as/in place of our invitations/right to enter (ENterANCE)
14 (1) look us up and down, (2) evaluate, appraise
15 give
16 dance★

Romeo   Give me a torch. I am not for this ambling.[17]

Being but heavy,[18] I will bear[19] the light.

Mercutio Nay, gentle Romeo, we must have you dance.

Romeo   Not I, believe me. You have dancing shoes

With nimble[20] soles, I have a soul of lead   15

So stakes[21] me to the ground I cannot move.

Mercutio You are a lover. Borrow Cupid's wings

And soar with them above a common bound.[22]

Romeo   I am too sore enpiercèd[23] with his shaft[24]

To soar with his light feathers,[25] and so bound[26]   20

I cannot bound a pitch above[27] dull[28] woe.

Under love's heavy burden do I sink.

Mercutio And, to sink in it, should you burden[29] love?

Too great oppression for a tender thing.[30]

Romeo   Is love a tender thing? It is too rough,   25

Too rude,[31] too boist'rous,[32] and it pricks like thorn.

Mercutio If love be rough with you, be rough with love.

17 easy-paced, sometimes artificial walking/dancing
18 oppressed, sorrowful
19 carry
20 quick, swift, agile, light
21 so stakes = which so fastens
22 (1) limit, (2) leap
23 sore enpiercèd = painfully/severely penetrated/run through
24 rod forming the body of an arrow
25 with his light feathers = as he does with the light feathers of his wings
26 fastened, tied down (adjective)
27 bound (verb) a pitch above = leap higher than
28 slow, stupid, sluggish, drowsy
29 (1) load, oppress, (2) criticize
30 a tender thing = (1) love, (2) a woman, bearing his weight in sexual
    intercourse (as he "sinks in" to her), (3) a woman's genitals
31 uncultivated, barbarous, harsh, violent★
32 (1) stiff, coarse, unyielding, (2) truculent, fierce, violent

Prick love for pricking,[33] and you beat love down.[34]
Give me a case[35] to put my visage[36] in.
30   A visor for a visor![37] What care I
What curious[38] eye doth quote[39] deformities?
Here[40] are the beetle brows[41] shall blush for me.

Benvolio   Come, knock and enter, and no sooner in
But every man betake him[42] to his legs.[43]

35   *Romeo*   A torch for me. Let wantons[44] light of heart
Tickle[45] the senseless[46] rushes[47] with their heels,
For I am proverbed[48] with a grandsire phrase:[49]
I'll be a candle holder[50] and look on.
The game[51] was ne'er so fair,[52] and I am done.[53]

---

33 (1) painfully sticking, (2) sexual intercourse (then as now the noun "prick" =
   vulgar term for penis)
34 beat love down = overthrow/force down love
35 holder, sheath
36 my visage = my assumed/pretend face/appearance (his mask)
37 a visor for a visor = a mask (disguise) for a mask (his face)
38 careful, attentive, fussy
39 mark, observe, scrutinize
40 in this mask
41 beetle brows = black, jutting eyebrows
42 commit himself, resort
43 to his legs = dance
44 those free of care/given to unrestrained merriment, frisky
45 poke, touch, stir up
46 incapable of feeling
47 dry reeds spread on floors
48 furnished with a proverb
49 grandsire phrase = proverb as old as a grandfather
50 "If a man does not know how to play at cards, it is kind of him to hold the
   candle"
51 (1) amusement, fun, (2) amorous play/sport
52 ne'er so fair = never so fair as it is now (and that being so, it is time to give it
   up)
53 finished, used up

Mercutio Tut! Dun's the mouse, the constable's own word.[54]   40

  If thou art Dun,[55] we'll draw thee from the mire[56]

  Of – save your reverence[57] – love, wherein thou stick'st[58]

  Up to the ears. Come, we burn daylight,[59] ho!

Romeo Nay, that's not so.

Mercutio   I mean, sir, in delay

  We waste our lights[60] in vain, like lamps by[61] day.   45

  Take our good meaning,[62] for our judgment sits[63]

  Five times in that[64] ere[65] once in our five wits.[66]

Romeo And we mean[67] well, in going to this masque.

  But 'tis no wit[68] to go.

---

54 Dun's the mouse, the constable's own word = a mouse is brown, and
  proverbially quiet, like an officer of the peace (Romeo has just said he is
  "*done*")

55 (Mercutio swiftly changes directions, referring now to Dun the horse in an
  old Christmas game: those playing the game try to pull a large, heavy log,
  supposed to be Dun the horse, out of an imaginary mire)

56 (1) boggy/swampy ground, (2) dirt, filth, dung

57 save your reverence = excuse me (Mercutio apologizes – or pretends to –
  for using so obscene and dirty a word as "mire" to describe love: some texts
  have "sirreverence," with the same meaning, but "sirreverence" can also
  mean human excrement/dung)

58 are stuck

59 burn daylight = delay, waste time

60 (1) torches, (2) feelings, (3) capacities ("lights" also = the lungs: waste our
  lights = waste our breath, jabbering like this)

61 lit/burning in daylight

62 take our good meaning = choose/understand our/my correct meaning
  (instead of pretending, as Romeo clearly does, that he does not understand)

63 judgment sits = deliberate opinion/good sense is located/can be found

64 five times in that = five times as much in that good meaning

65 in preference to, rather than in

66 once in our five wits = one time in what we learn via our five senses
  ("wits")

67 intend (Romeo changes verbal direction every bit as swiftly, and lightly, as
  does Mercutio)

68 not sensible/wise/clever

Mercutio	Why, may one ask?
Romeo	I dreamt a dream tonight.[69]
Mercutio	And so did I.
Romeo	Well, what was yours?
Mercutio	That dreamers often lie.
Romeo	In bed asleep, while they do dream things true.
Mercutio	O, then I see Queen Mab[70] hath been with you.

She is the fairies' midwife,[71] and she comes

In shape no bigger than an agate stone

On the forefinger of an alderman,[72]

Drawn[73] with a team of little atomies

Athwart[74] men's noses as they lie asleep —[75]

Her wagon spokes made of long spinners'[76] legs,

The cover,[77] of the wings of grasshoppers;

Her traces,[78] of the smallest spider's web;

Her collars,[79] of the moonshine's wat'ry[80] beams;

Her whip, of cricket's bone; the lash,[81] of film;[82]

---

69 last night
70 (an invented personage, probably meant to be "mythological/fairy"; but mab = slut, whore)
71 (it is she, among the fairies, who "delivers" their dreams to humans)
72 (the figures of diminutive persons were cut into agate stones, mounted on rings used for affixing seals on letters and other documents; aldermen were headmen/governors of trade organizations and municipal districts)
73 (Mab is drawn by a team of tiny creatures the size of atoms)
74 across
75 (the next eleven lines are differently ordered in some texts)
76 spiders'
77 outer covering of the wheels
78 straps/ropes connecting the collar of the drawing/pulling animal to the whiffletree/crossbar of the vehicle
79 her "horses"/draft animals' collars
80 (1) moist, (2) thin, (3) pale
81 flexible tip of a whip
82 membrane, filament, gossamer (spider webs?)

Her wagoner, a small gray-coated[83] gnat,

Not half so big as a round little worm 65

Pricked from the lazy finger of a maid;[84]

Her chariot is an empty hazelnut,

Made by the joiner[85] squirrel or old grub,[86]

Time out o' mind the fairies' coachmakers.

And in this state[87] she gallops night by night 70

Through lovers' brains, and then they dream of love;

O'er courtiers'[88] knees, that dream on curtsies[89] straight;[90]

O'er lawyers' fingers, who straight dream on fees;

O'er ladies' lips, who straight on kisses dream,

Which[91] oft the angry Mab with blisters plagues,[92] 75

Because their breaths with sweetmeats[93] tainted[94] are.

Sometime she gallops o'er a courtier's nose,

And then dreams he of smelling out a suit;[95]

And sometime comes she with a tithe pig's[96] tail

Tickling a parson's nose as 'a lies asleep, 80

Then dreams he of another benefice.[97]

---

83 gray-coated = a uniform? a reference to traditional homespun cloth?

84 serving maid (lazy serving maids were said to breed tiny worms in their fingers)

85 cabinetmaker

86 (squirrels *gnaw;* worm grubs *bore*)

87 pomp, splendor, exalted position/rank, greatness

88 those who congregate at a sovereign's court

89 gestures of respect, made by bending one's knees

90 without delay, immediately

91 who

92 (verb)

93 candies, cakes, etc.

94 contaminated, corrupted, stained

95 smelling out a suit = discovering some cause for a lawsuit? or a patron who will pay for his influence at court?

96 tithe pig = animal given as/in lieu of tithe money

97 salaried church post

Sometimes she driveth o'er a soldier's neck,
And then dreams he of cutting foreign throats,
Of breaches,[98] ambuscadoes,[99] Spanish blades,[100]
85   Of healths[101] five fathom deep; and then anon[102]
Drums[103] in his ear, at which he starts[104] and wakes,
And being thus frighted swears a prayer or two
And sleeps again. This is that very Mab
That plats[105] the manes of horses in the night
90   And bakes[106] the elflocks[107] in foul sluttish[108] hair,
Which once untangled much misfortune bodes.[109]
This is the hag,[110] when maids lie on their backs,
That presses them and learns[111] them first to bear,[112]
Making them women of good carriage.[113]
This is she –

95 *Romeo*   Peace,[114] peace, Mercutio, peace!
Thou talk'st of nothing.

    Mercutio   True, I talk of dreams,

---

98 breaks in fortified walls
99 ambushes
100 swords (made of superior steel)
101 alcoholic toasts/pledges
102 at once★
103 she drums (verb)
104 is startled
105 plaits, intertwines
106 hardens, cakes
107 mass of tangled hair, caused in one's sleep by malicious elves
108 dirty, untidy
109 forebodes, promises (because it will anger the elves?)
110 female evil spirit/demon
111 instructs, teaches
112 (1) bear a lover's weight, (2) behave, walk, (3) bear children
113 of good carriage = of good bearing/capacity to carry
114 enough! quiet!

Which are the children of an idle[115] brain,

Begot[116] of nothing but vain[117] fantasy,[118]

Which is as thin of substance[119] as the air,

And more inconstant than the wind, who woos   100

Even now the frozen bosom[120] of the North

And, being angered,[121] puffs[122] away from thence,

Turning his face[123] to the dew-dropping South.

Benvolio   This wind you talk of blows us from ourselves.[124]

Supper is done, and we shall come too late.   105

Romeo   I fear too early; for my mind misgives[125]

Some consequence,[126] yet hanging[127] in the stars,[128]

Shall bitterly begin his[129] fearful[130] date

With this night's revels and expire[131] the term

Of a despisèd life, closed[132] in my breast,   110

By some vile forfeit[133] of untimely[134] death.

---

115 empty, vacant★
116 generated, created
117 empty, vacant, worthless
118 illusory/imaginary appearance
119 solid/real matter★
120 seat of emotions/desires, heart
121 (because it is frozen/cold)
122 blows abruptly/quickly/hard
123 (some texts have "side")
124 from ourselves = away from our purpose/direction
125 suggests, fears
126 future result/event
127 yet hanging = even now pending
128 astrologically/fatefully determined
129 its
130 dreadful, terrible, awful
131 finish, end, conclude
132 shut, contained
133 vile forfeit = (1)base/low/horrid/despicable penalty, (2)contractually agreed-upon large additional penalty (for nonpayment)
134 premature★

But he that hath the steerage[135] of my course[136]
Direct my sail! On, lusty gentlemen!
Benvolio Strike, drum.[137]

THEY MARCH TO ONE SIDE OF THE STAGE, AND STAND THERE

135 steering, guidance
136 path, direction of onward movement★
137 drummer (a man leading the celebrants)

SCENE 5
Capulet's house

SERVINGMEN COME FORTH WITH NAPKINS[1]

First Servingman   Where's Potpan, that he helps not to take
away? He shift[2] a trencher![3] He scrape[4] a trencher!

Second Servingman   When good manners shall lie all in one or
two men's hands, and they unwashed too, 'tis a foul thing.

First Servingman   Away with the joint stools,[5] remove the   5
court cupboard,[6] look to[7] the plate.[8] Good[9] thou, save me a
piece of marchpane[10] and, as thou loves me, let[11] the porter
let in Susan Grindstone and Nell. – (*calling*) Anthony and
Potpan!

[12]*Second Servingman* Ay, boy, ready.   10

First Servingman   You are looked for and called for, asked for
and sought for, in the great chamber.[13]

Third Servingman   We cannot be here and there too.

---

1 "'It is equally impolite to lick greasy fingers or to wipe them on one's tunic,'
wrote Erasmus in 1530. 'You should wipe them with the napkin or on the
tablecloth.'" Visser, *The Rituals of Dinner,* 163
2 arrange, distribute
3 flat wooden platters, in the next century replaced by plates
4 scrape off, clean
5 joint stools = stools professionally made by a joiner/cabinetmaker
6 court cupboard = sideboard
7 look to = (1) attend to, take care of, (2) be careful of★
8 silver or gold utensils
9 (friendly/familiar)
10 marzipan
11 cause
12 (this and the next two speeches are attributed differently in some texts)
13 great chamber = main hall?

Cheerly,[14] boys! Be brisk[15] awhile,[16] and the longer liver take
15 all.[17]

ENTER CAPULET, LADY CAPULET, JULIET, TYBALT,
NURSE, GUESTS, AND GENTLEWOMEN

Capulet   (*to Maskers*) Welcome, gentlemen. Ladies that have
their toes
Unplagued[18] with corns will walk a bout[19] with you.
Ah, my mistresses,[20] which of you all
Will now deny to[21] dance? She that makes dainty,[22]
20 She I'll swear hath corns.[23] Am I come near[24] ye now?
(*to Maskers*) Welcome, gentlemen. I have seen the day
That I have worn a visor[25] and could tell
A whispering tale in a fair lady's ear,
Such as would please. 'Tis gone, 'tis gone, 'tis gone.
25 You are welcome, gentlemen. Come, musicians, play.

MUSIC. THEY DANCE

A hall, a hall![26] Give room! And foot it,[27] girls.

14 (1) lively, (2) cheerily
15 quick, active
16 for a short time
17 the longer liver take all = enjoy yourselves, make the most of the present
(proverbial)
18 not cursed/afflicted
19 walk a bout = move/make a turn/circuit
20 my mistresses = my ladies ("mistress": polite form of address)
21 deny to = refuse to
22 reluctant, disinclined
23 bunions
24 am I come near = have I come close to/reached/touched
25 mask
26 a hall! = make room, clear the floor
27 foot it = on with the dancing

More light, you knaves,[28] and turn the tables up,[29]
And quench the fire, the room is grown too hot.
(*to Capulet Old Man*) Ah, sirrah, this unlooked-for sport[30]
comes[31] well.
Nay, sit, nay sit, good cousin Capulet,   30
For you and I are past our dancing days.
How long is't now since last yourself and I
Were in a mask?[32]

Second Capulet   By'r Lady, thirty years.

Capulet   What, man? 'Tis not so much, 'tis not so much.
'Tis since the nuptial[33] of Lucentio,   35
Come Pentecost[34] as quickly as it will,[35]
Some five-and-twenty years, and then we masked.

Second Capulet 'Tis more, 'tis more. His[36] son is older, sir,
His son is thirty.

Capulet   Will you tell me that?
His son was but a ward[37] two years ago.   40

Romeo   (*to Servingman*) What lady's that, which doth
enrich[38] the hand[39]
Of yonder knight?

28 male servants
29 turn the tables up = lift the flat tops off their supporting trestles/sawhorses,
   and stack them against the wall
30 entertainment, amusement, recreation
31 presents itself, arrives, happens, turns out
32 were in a mask = (1) wore a mask, (2) were at a masquerade dance
33 wedding
34 seventh Sunday after Easter ("Whitsuntide")
35 wants to
36 Lucentio's son
37 under age twenty-one, a minor
38 decorate, adorn
39 (the man's hand holding hers, presumably, in the course of dancing)

Servingman I know not, sir.

Romeo O she doth teach the torches to burn[40] bright.

45 It seems she hangs upon[41] the cheek of night
Like a rich jewel in an Ethiop's ear[42] –
Beauty too rich[43] for use,[44] for earth too dear.[45]
So shows[46] a snowy dove trooping[47] with crows
As yonder lady o'er[48] her fellows shows.

50 The measure done, I'll watch her place of stand[49]
And, touching hers,[50] make blessèd my rude hand.
Did my heart love till now? Forswear[51] it, sight.
For I ne'er saw true beauty till this night.[52]

Tybalt This, by his voice, should be a Montague.

55 *(to Servant)* Fetch me my rapier,[53] boy. What, dares the slave
Come hither, covered with an antic[54] face,
To fleer[55] and scorn[56] at our solemnity?[57]
Now by the stock[58] and honor of my kin,

---

40 to burn = how properly to burn
41 hangs upon = is suspended on, decorates
42 (bright/glittering objects are seen more vividly against a dark background)
43 great, exalted, noble, splendid, fine, luxurious
44 for use = to be used/usefully employed
45 (1) precious, valuable, costly, (2) scarce, unusual
46 appears/is displayed/seen/exhibited
47 that flocks/gathers/associates with
48 higher than, beyond, in preference/comparison to
49 her place of stand = where she stands
50 her hand
51 renounce, repudiate
52 (for I ne'er SAW true BEAUty TILL this NIGHT)
53 light, sharp-pointed sword
54 grinning, fantastic (Romeo's mask)
55 jeer, gibe, laugh contemptuously
56 treat with ridicule, mock
57 ceremony, special formality, festival
58 line of descent, pedigree, genealogy

To strike him dead I hold[59] it not a sin.

Capulet Why, how now, kinsman? Wherefore storm[60] you so? 60

Tybalt   Uncle, this is a Montague, our foe,

A villain that is hither come in spite[61]

To scorn at our solemnity this night.

Capulet Young Romeo is it?

Tybalt   'Tis he, that villain Romeo.

Capulet Content thee,[62] gentle coz, let him alone. 65

'A bears him like a portly[63] gentleman,

And, to say truth, Verona brags of him

To be a virtuous and well-governed[64] youth.

I would not for the wealth of all this town

Here in my house do him disparagement.[65] 70

Therefore be patient, take no note of him.

It is my will, the which if thou respect,

Show a fair presence[66] and put off these frowns,

An ill-beseeming semblance[67] for a feast.

Tybalt   It fits when such a villain is a guest. 75

I'll not endure him.

Capulet   He shall be endured.

What, goodman boy![68] I say he shall. Go to![69]

59 think, consider, believe*
60 wherefore storm = why* rage
61 envious malice / hatred, contemptuously
62 content thee = be satisfied
63 dignified
64 well-governed = reasonable
65 dishonor, indignity
66 appearance, bearing, demeanor
67 appearance
68 (used for people of rank lower than gentleman; "boy" also is deliberately
   insulting)
69 come on! (exclamation of incredulity and disapproval)

Am I the master here, or you? Go to!

You'll not endure him? God shall mend my soul![70]

80   You'll make a mutiny[71] among my guests,

You will set cock-a-hoop,[72] you'll be the man![73]

Tybalt Why, uncle, 'tis a shame.[74]

Capulet   Go to, go to!

You are a saucy[75] boy. Is't so,[76] indeed?

This trick[77] may chance to scathe[78] you. I know what.[79]

85   You must contrary[80] me! Marry, 'tis time –

(*to Dancers*) Well said, my hearts![81]—(*to Tybalt*) You are a

princox,[82] go

Be quiet, or – (*to Servingmen*) More light, more light! – (*to*

Tybalt) For shame!

I'll make you quiet. What! – (*to Dancers*) Cheerly, my hearts!

Tybalt Patience perforce[83] with wilful choler[84] meeting

90   Makes my flesh tremble in their different greeting.[85]

---

70 God shall mend my soul! = May God purify my soul! (emphatic
   exclamation)
71 quarrel, disturbance
72 set cock-a-hoop = cast off all restraint, set everything by the ears
73 be the man! = be in charge, give the orders
74 disgrace, dishonor
75 insolent, presumptuous★
76 is't so? = is that the way it is?
77 prank, mischief, frolic
78 hurt, injure, damage
79 I know what = I understand what I'm doing, I'm not a fool/incompetent (I
   know WHAT) (and you don't!)
80 oppose, strive against (conTRAry)
81 (term of endearment)
82 conceited young man
83 (1) forcibly, (2) of necessity, under compulsion★
84 wilful choler = obstinately self-willed/irrational/perverse temper/anger
85 in their different greeting = because of the totally unlike and clashing
   natures of patience and choler

I will withdraw. But this intrusion[86] shall,

Now seeming sweet, convert to[87] bitt'rest gall.[88]

EXIT

Romeo   If I profane[89] with my unworthiest hand

This holy shrine,[90] the gentle sin is this:

My lips, two blushing[91] pilgrims,[92] ready stand   95

To smooth that[93] rough touch with a tender[94] kiss.

Juliet   Good pilgrim, you do wrong[95] your hand too much,

Which[96] mannerly devotion[97] shows in this,

For saints[98] have hands that pilgrims' hands do touch,

And palm to palm is holy palmers'[99] kiss.   100

Romeo   Have not saints lips, and holy palmers too?

Juliet   Ay, pilgrim, lips that they must use in prayer.

Romeo   O, then, dear saint, let lips do what hands do.

They pray: grant thou,[100] lest faith turn to despair.

Juliet   Saints do not move,[101] though grant for prayers'   105

---

86 (Romeo's uninvited presence)
87 convert to = turn into
88 (1) rancor, (2) poison, venom
89 desecrate, pollute, treat irreverently
90 (her hand – which, as he had earlier said he would, he is now holding)
91 (1) reddish in color, (2) modest
92 (like religious pilgrims, he has sought out a sacred place)
93 (his own)
94 soft, gentle
95 (verb)
96 and that
97 mannerly devotion = decent/ moral/ modest and devout reverence/ impulse/observance/prayer
98 (1) holy persons, (2) those who are among the chosen, (3) statues of saints
99 pilgrims'
100 grant thou = that prayer (that I may kiss your lips)
101 (1) commence, start, (2) speak, (3) become agitated, disturbed, (4) move (if "saints" means a statue)

sake.[102]

Romeo   Then move not while my prayer's effect[103] I take.

Thus from my lips, by thine my sin is purged.[104] (*kisses her*)

Juliet   Then[105] have my lips the sin that they have took.

Romeo   Sin from my lips? O trespass[106] sweetly urged![107]

Give me my sin again. (*kisses her*)

110 *Juliet*   You kiss by th' book.[108]

Nurse   Madam, your mother craves[109] a word with you.

Romeo   What[110] is her mother?

Nurse   Marry, bachelor,[111]

Her mother is the lady of the house,

And a good lady, and a wise and virtuous.

115   I nursed her daughter that you talked withal.[112]

I tell you, he that can lay hold of her

Shall have the chinks.[113]

Romeo   Is she a Capulet?

O dear account.[114] My life is my foe's debt.[115]

---

102 though grant for prayer's sake = though they may, in response to a prayer, grant what is requested

103 result

104 cleansed, purified, absolved

105 as a result, now

106 sin, fault, wrong (noun)

107 brought forward, presented, stated

108 (1) book of manners, (2) book of sonnets (till the moment he kisses her, their dialogue is a sonnet)

109 (1) demands, claims by authority/right, (2) requests, (3) wants*

110 who

111 young gentleman

112 with

113 money (that which "chinks": coins – there being no paper money)

114 dear account = costly/dire/grievous reckoning

115 (she is his "foe," but his life is owed to her)

Benvolio Away, be gone, the sport is at the best.[116]

Romeo Ay, so I fear: the more is my unrest.[117]   120

Capulet Nay, gentlemen, prepare not[118] to be gone.

We have a trifling foolish[119] banquet[120] towards.[121]

(*they whisper in his ear*) Is it e'en so? Why then, I thank you all,

I thank you, honest[122] gentlemen. Good night.

(*to Servingmen*) More torches here! (*Maskers leave*) Come on

then, let's to bed.   125

Ah, sirrah, by my fay,[123] it waxes[124] late.

I'll to my rest.

EXEUNT ALL BUT JULIET AND NURSE

Juliet Come hither, Nurse. What is yond gentleman?[125]

Nurse The son and heir of old Tiberio.

Juliet What's he that now is going out of door?   130

Nurse Marry, that, I think, be young Petruchio.

Juliet What's he that follows there, that would not dance?

Nurse I know not.

Juliet Go ask his name. − (*to herself*) If he be marrièd,

My grave is like[126] to be my wedding bed.   135

Nurse His name is Romeo, and a Montague,

---

116 see act 1, scene 4, note 52
117 turmoil
118 prepare not = don't ready yourselves
119 trifling foolish = insignificant/petty/humble
120 small repast/meal
121 on the way
122 honorable*
123 faith (a common exclamation)
124 grows
125 yond gentleman = that distant gentleman (over there)
126 likely

The only son of your great enemy.

Juliet   My only love, sprung from my only hate.

Too early seen unknown, and known too late.

140   Prodigious[127] birth of love it is to me

That I must love a loathèd enemy.

Nurse   What's this? what's this?

Juliet   A rhyme I learnt even now

Of one I danced withal.

A CALL WITHIN: JULIET

Nurse   Anon, anon!

Come, let's away; the strangers all are gone.

EXEUNT

127 (1) ominous, unnatural, monstrous, (2) astonishing, amazing

Act 2

PROLOGUE

ENTER CHORUS

Chorus Now old desire[1] doth in his[2] deathbed lie,
    And young affection gapes[3] to be his[4] heir.
    That fair[5] for which love groaned for and would die,[6]
    With tender Juliet matched[7] is now not fair.
    Now Romeo is beloved, and loves again,   5
    Alike[8] bewitchèd by the charm of looks,[9]
    But to his foe[10] supposed[11] he must complain[12]

---

1 old desire = Romeo's former love
2 its
3 is eager
4 its
5 Rosaline
6 would die = (1) wished to die, (2) wished for sexual orgasm
7 compared
8 both Romeo and Juliet
9 (once again, see act 1, scene 2, note 47)
10 (1) enemy, as a Capulet, (2) female belovèd, in Renaissance love poetry
11 erroneously believed (referring to meaning 1, in note 10, just above)
12 lament, moan, mourn (in a literary sense)

53

And she steal[13] love's sweet bait[14] from fearful hooks.[15]
Being held[16] a foe, he may not have access
10 To breathe[17] such vows as lovers use to[18] swear,
And she as much in love, her means[19] much less
To meet her new belovèd anywhere.
 But passion lends them power, time means, to meet,
Tempering[20] extremities with extreme sweet.

EXIT

13 take secretly
14 allurement, temptation
15 fearful hooks = dreadful/terrible snares, traps
16 believed to be
17 speak, passionately utter/whisper
18 use to = customarily
19 resources, possibilities for action★
20 mingling, modifying

SCENE I

A lane outside the wall of Capulet's orchard[21]

ENTER ROMEO

Romeo Can I go forward[22] when my heart is here?
  Turn back, dull earth,[23] and find thy center[24] out.[25]

HE CLIMBS THE WALL AND LEAPS DOWN THE OTHER SIDE

ENTER BENVOLIO AND MERCUTIO

Benvolio Romeo! My cousin Romeo! Romeo!
Mercutio   He's wise,
  And, on my life, hath stol'n[26] him home to bed.
Benvolio He ran this way, and leapt this orchard wall.   5
  Call, good Mercutio.
Mercutio   Nay, I'll conjure[27] too.
  (*loudly*) Romeo! Humors! Madman! Passion! Lover!
  Appear thou in the likeness of a sigh.
  Speak but one rhyme, and I am satisfied.
  Cry but "Ay me!" Pronounce but "love"' and "dove."   10
  Speak to my gossip[28] Venus one fair word,
  One nickname for her purblind[29] son and heir,

21 garden
22 go forward = move on
23 earth = Romeo's body (humans having been created from earth/dust)
24 she around whom his life revolves (Juliet)
25 find . . . out = search for
26 gone secretly
27 (1) invoke magically sacred names, (2) beseech
28 intimate/chatty friend
29 totally blind

Young Abraham[30] Cupid, he that shot so trim[31]

When King Cophetua[32] loved the beggar maid.

15   (*pause*) He[33] heareth not, he stirreth not, he moveth not.

The ape is dead,[34] and I must conjure him.

(*loudly*) I conjure thee by Rosaline's bright eyes,

By her high forehead and her scarlet lip,

By her fine foot, straight leg, and quivering thigh,

20   And the demesnes[35] that there adjacent[36] lie,

That in thy likeness thou appear to us!

Benvolio   An if he hear thee, thou wilt anger him.

Mercutio   This cannot anger him. 'Twould anger him

To raise a spirit[37] in his mistress' circle[38]

25   Of some strange nature, letting it there stand[39]

Till she had laid it[40] and conjured it down.[41]

That were some[42] spite. My invocation

Is fair and honest: in his mistress' name,

---

30 young Abraham = young old

31 fine, beautifully

32 ("King Cophetua and the Beggar Maid" = old ballad in which a king, hostile to love, is looking out the window at a beggar maid, when Cupid, "The blinded boy, that shoots so trim," hits the king with an arrow. Cophetua falls in love and eventually marries the beggar girl. See Percy, *Reliques of Ancient English Poetry,* 1:189–94. The king's name is pronounced coFETya)

33 Romeo

34 ape is dead = Romeo is playing dead, as performing apes were trained to do

35 regions (usually used for land, territories: diMEENZ)

36 bordering, close by (meaning, here, "genitalia")

37 (1) supernatural being, demon (2) vital power, penis

38 (1) magic cirle, used for conjuring, (2) genitalia

39 be erect (bawdy)

40 laid it = (1) set it to rest (2) had sexual intercourse with it

41 (1) back to hell, (2) no longer erect (bawdy)

42 considerable

I conjure only but to raise up him.[43]

Benvolio   Come, he hath hid himself among these trees   30

To be consorted[44] with the humorous[45] night.

Blind is his love and best befits[46] the dark.

Mercutio   If love be blind, love cannot hit the mark.

Now will he sit under a medlar[47] tree

And wish his mistress were that kind of fruit   35

As maids call medlars when they laugh alone.[48]

O Romeo, that she were, O that she were

An open arse,[49] thou[50] a pop'rin pear![51]

Romeo, good night. I'll to my truckle bed.[52]

This field bed is too cold for me to sleep.   40

Come, shall we go?

Benvolio   Go then, for 'tis in vain

To seek him here that means not to be found.

EXEUNT

43 (bawdy)
44 united, in harmony
45 moody, capricious
46 suited for
47 a kind of apple, edible only when ripe enough to burst; thought to resemble
    female genitalia
48 (with no men present)
49 (1) medlar fruit, (2) posterior, rump ("arse" = British form of "ass")
50 and you were
51 a kind of pear, shaped like a penis
52 truckle bed = bed on castors/wheels

SCENE 2
Capulet's orchard

ENTER ROMEO

Romeo He[1] jests at scars that[2] never felt a wound.

ENTER JULIET ABOVE, AT A WINDOW

(*quietly*) But soft. What light through yonder window breaks?

It is the East, and Juliet is the sun.

Arise, fair sun, and kill the envious moon,

5 Who is already sick and pale with grief

That thou her maid art far more fair than she.

Be not her maid,[3] since she is envious.

Her vestal livery[4] is but sick[5] and green,[6]

And none but fools[7] do wear it. Cast it off.

10 It is my lady![8] O it is my love.

O that she knew she were.[9]

She speaks,[10] yet she says nothing. What of that?

Her eye discourses:[11] I will answer it.

I am too bold. 'Tis not to me she speaks.

15 Two of the fairest stars in all the heaven,

1 Mercutio: Romeo hears him from the other side of the wall
2 who
3 be not her maid = (1) don't serve her, (2) don't remain a virgin
4 vestal livery = virginal clothing, servants' uniform★
5 pale, wan
6 ("green sickness" = anemia common to pubescent young women)
7 court jesters, who wore green and yellow coats
8 adored woman (chivalric term)
9 was my lady
10 is affecting/expressive
11 speaks, talks

Having some business, do entreat her eyes
To twinkle in their spheres[12] till they return.
What if her eyes were there,[13] they[14] in her head?
The brightness of her cheek would shame those stars
As daylight doth a lamp. Her eyes in heaven   20
Would through the airy region stream so bright
That birds would sing and think it were[15] not night.
See how she leans her cheek upon her hand.
O that I were a glove upon that hand,
That I might touch that cheek.

Juliet   Ay me.

Romeo   She speaks.   25
O speak again,[16] bright angel, for thou art
As glorious to this night, being o'er my head,[17]
As is a wingèd messenger[18] of heaven
Unto the white upturnèd wond'ring eyes
Of mortals that fall back[19] to gaze on him,   30
When he bestrides[20] the lazy puffing[21] clouds
And sails upon the bosom[22] of the air.

Juliet   O Romeo, Romeo, wherefore[23] art thou Romeo?

12 (in Ptolemaic astronomy, stars were contained in spheres)
13 in the sky
14 the stars
15 (subjunctive)
16 (Romeo is still talking, quietly, to himself only)
17 (Juliet is at her window, which is "above" stage level)
18 wingèd messenger = angel
19 fall back = retreat, step back
20 he bestrides = the angel mounts/rides on
21 sending out wisps/vapors (some texts have "pacing")
22 surface
23 wherefore art thou = why are you (named)

Deny[24] thy father and refuse thy name.

35   Or, if thou wilt not, be but sworn[25] my love

And I'll no longer be a Capulet.[26]

Romeo   (*aside*) Shall I hear more, or shall I speak at this?

Juliet   'Tis but thy name that is my enemy:

Thou art thyself, though not a Montague.

40   What's Montague? It is nor[27] hand nor foot,

Nor arm, nor face, nor any other part

Belonging to a man. O be some other name.[28]

What's in a name? That which we call a rose

By any other name[29] would smell as sweet.

45   So Romeo would, were he not Romeo called,

Retain that dear[30] perfection which he owes[31]

Without that title.[32] Romeo, doff[33] thy name,

And for[34] that name, which is no part of thee,

Take all myself.

Romeo   (*speaking to her*) I take thee at thy word.

50   Call me but love, and I'll be new baptized,

Henceforth I never will be Romeo.

---

24 renounce, disavow, repudiate
25 (once Romeo swears that he is her love, and intends to marry her, she will consider herself married)
26 (since a married woman takes her husband's name)
27 neither
28 beLONGing to a MAN o BE some OTHer NAME ("to a" are partly elided words, just barely syllables)
29 (some texts have "word")
30 noble, glorious★
31 possesses, owns
32 name
33 lay aside, get rid of
34 in place / instead of

Juliet   What man[35] art thou that, thus bescreened[36] in night,
So stumblest on[37] my counsel?[38]

Romeo   By a name
I know not how to tell thee who I am.
My name, dear saint, is hateful to myself,   55
Because it is an enemy to thee.
Had I it written, I would tear[39] the word.

Juliet   My ears have yet not drunk a hundred words
Of that tongue's utterance,[40] yet I know the sound.
Art thou not Romeo, and a Montague?   60

Romeo   Neither, fair saint, if either thee dislike.[41]

Juliet   How cam'st thou hither, tell me, and wherefore?
The orchard walls are high and hard to climb,
And the place death, considering who thou art,
If any of my kinsmen find thee here.   65

Romeo   With love's light wings did I o'erperch[42] these walls,
For stony limits[43] cannot hold love out,
And what love can do, that dares love attempt.
Therefore thy kinsmen are no let[44] to me.

Juliet   If they do see thee, they will murder thee.   70

Romeo   Alack, there lies more peril in thine eye
Than twenty of their swords. Look thou but sweet,

35 what man = who
36 hidden from sight, covered in darkness
37 stumblest on = comes upon accidentally/by chance
38 private musing
39 take away/remove by force/violence
40 UTrance
41 offend, displease
42 fly over
43 boundaries
44 barrier, stop (some texts have "stop")

And I am proof[45] against their enmity.

Juliet   I would not for the world they saw thee here.

75 *Romeo* I have night's cloak to hide me from their sight,

And but[46] thou love me, let them find me here.

My life were better ended by their hate

Than death proroguèd,[47] wanting of[48] thy love.

Juliet   By whose direction[49] found'st thou out this place?

80 *Romeo* By love, that first did prompt[50] me to inquire.

He[51] lent me counsel,[52] and I lent him eyes.

I am no pilot,[53] yet wert thou as far[54]

As that vast shore washed with[55] the farthest sea,

I would adventure[56] for such merchandise.

85 *Juliet*   Thou knowest the mask of night is on my face,

Else would a maiden blush bepaint my cheek

For that which thou hast heard me speak tonight.

Fain[57] would I dwell on form[58] – fain, fain deny

What I have spoke. But farewell compliment.[59]

90   Dost thou love me? I know thou wilt say "Ay,"

---

45 impenetrable, invulnerable
46 if only
47 deferred, postponed
48 wanting of = lacking, without
49 guidance, giving of directions
50 incite, urge, inspire
51 Love/Cupid
52 advice
53 steersman, helmsman, versed in local navigation
54 far away
55 (1) washed with = bathed/wet by/beat upon by, (2) adjoining, touching
56 take the chance/the risk, venture★
57 gladly★
58 dwell on form = linger/insist on formality/decorum/etiquette
59 ceremony, politeness

And I will take thy word. Yet, if thou swear'st,
Thou mayst prove false. At lovers' perjuries,
They say Jove[60] laughs. O gentle Romeo,
If thou dost love, pronounce it faithfully.[61]
Or if thou thinkest I am too quickly won,   95
I'll frown, and be perverse,[62] and say thee nay,
So[63] thou wilt woo.[64] But else,[65] not for the world.
In truth, fair Montague, I am too fond,[66]
And therefore thou mayst think my havior[67] light,[68]
But trust me, gentleman, I'll prove more true[69]   100
Than those that have more cunning[70] to be strange.[71]
I should have been more strange, I must confess,
But that thou overheard'st, ere I was ware,[72]
My true love[73] passion. Therefore pardon me,
And not impute this yielding to light love,   105
Which[74] the dark night hath so discoverèd.[75]
Romeo Lady, by yonder blessèd moon I swear,

60 king of the gods
61 in truth, sincerely
62 stubborn, difficult
63 in order that
64 court me
65 otherwise
66 foolishly tender, over-affectionate, doting*
67 behavior, conduct, deportment
68 wanton, frivolous, not to be respected
69 faithful, reliable, steadfast*
70 capacity, skill
71 distant, reserved, cold
72 aware, conscious
73 (adjective)
74 this love which
75 uncovered, disclosed, revealed

That tips[76] with silver all these fruit tree tops –

Juliet   O swear not by the moon, th' inconstant[77] moon,

110   That monthly changes in her circled orb,[78]

Lest that thy love prove likewise variable.

Romeo   What shall I swear by?

Juliet   Do not swear at all,

Or if thou wilt, swear by thy gracious[79] self,

Which is the god of my idolatry,[80]

And I'll believe thee.

115 *Romeo*   If my heart's dear love –

Juliet   Well, do not swear. Although I joy[81] in thee,

I have no joy of this contract[82] tonight.

It is too rash,[83] too unadvised,[84] too sudden,

Too like the lightning, which doth cease to be

120   Ere one can say "It lightens."[85] Sweet, good night.

This bud of love, by summer's ripening breath,

May prove a beauteous flower when next we meet.

Good night, good night. As[86] sweet repose and rest

Come to thy heart as that within my breast.

125 *Romeo*   O wilt thou leave me so unsatisfied?

76 adorns
77 frequently changing/altering
78 circled orb = circular orbit
79 charming, attractive
80 idol worship
81 rejoice, delight, exult
82 mutual agreement (conTRACT)
83 hasty, impetuous, rapid
84 spoken without proper thought/reflection
85 flashes
86 the same, equal

Juliet   What satisfaction[87] canst thou have tonight?

Romeo   Th' exchange of thy love's faithful vow for mine.

Juliet   I gave thee mine before thou didst request it,

And yet I would[88] it were[89] to give again.

Romeo   Would'st thou withdraw it? For what purpose, love?   130

Juliet   But to be frank[90] and give it thee again.

And yet I wish but for the thing I have.

My bounty[91] is as boundless as the sea,

My love as deep. The more I give to thee,

The more I have, for both[92] are infinite.   135

I hear some noise within. Dear love, adieu!

NURSE CALLS WITHIN

Anon, good Nurse! – Sweet Montague, be true.

Stay but a little, I will come again.

EXIT JULIET

Romeo   O blessèd, blessèd night! I am afeard,

Being in night, all this is but a dream,   140

Too flattering[93] sweet to be substantial.[94]

ENTER JULIET ABOVE

---

87 gratification of desire (Juliet consistently shows a keen awareness of sexual realities)
88 wish
89 still remained
90 generous, lavish
91 generosity, liberality
92 what I have and what I give
93 pleasingly, pleasurably
94 real (subSTANtiAL)

<pre>
Juliet   Three words, dear Romeo, and good night indeed.[95]
          If that thy bent[96] of love be honorable,
          Thy purpose marriage, send me word tomorrow,
145   By one that I'll procure[97] to come to thee,
          Where and what time thou wilt perform the rite,
          And all my fortunes at thy foot I'll lay
          And follow thee my lord[98] throughout the world.
Nurse   (within) Madam!
150 Juliet   I come, anon. – But if thou meanest not well,
          I do beseech thee –
Nurse   (within) Madam!
Juliet   By and by[99] I come –
          To cease thy suit and leave me to my grief.
          Tomorrow will I send.
Romeo   So thrive[100] my soul –
Juliet   A thousand times good night.
</pre>

EXIT JULIET

<pre>
155 Romeo A thousand times the worse, to want[101] thy light.
          Love goes toward love as schoolboys from[102] their books,
          But love from[103] love, towards school[104] with heavy looks.
</pre>

ENTER JULIET ABOVE

95 really, positively
96 disposition, inclination
97 contrive, cause, get
98 husband (with the clear sense of "head of the household")
99 by and by = immediately, at once
100 flourish, prosper
101 lack*
102 go away from
103 away from
104 as schoolboys go

Juliet   Hist! Romeo, hist! O for a falconer's[105] voice
   To lure this tassel-gentle[106] back again.
   Bondage[107] is hoarse[108] and may not speak aloud,   160
   Else would I tear the cave where Echo lies[109]
   And make her airy tongue more hoarse than mine
   With repetition of my Romeo's name.
   Romeo!
Romeo   (*to himself*) It is my soul that calls upon my name.   165
   How silver sweet sound[110] lovers' tongues by night,
   Like softest music to attending ears.
Juliet   Romeo!
Romeo   My niesse.[111]
Juliet   What o'clock tomorrow
   Shall I send to thee?
Romeo   By the hour of nine.
Juliet   I will not fail. 'Tis twenty years till then.   170
   I have forgot why I did call thee back.
Romeo   Let me stand here till thou remember it.
Juliet   I shall forget, to have[112] thee still stand there,
   Rememb'ring how I love thy company.
Romeo   And I'll still stay, to have thee still forget,   175
   Forgetting any other home but this.
Juliet   'Tis almost morning. I would have thee gone,

---

105 keeper/trainer/hunter with falcons/hawks (who must call so high-flying
   birds can hear)
106 male falcon, nobler than a mere goshawk
107 restriction (as a young unmarried woman)
108 pitched low, not clear/smooth
109 (See Ovid, *Metamorphoses,* book 3)
110 (verb)
111 falcon/hawk too young to have flown (some texts have "nyas")
112 to have = in order to have

And yet no farther than a wanton's bird,[113]
That lets it hop a little from his hand,
180   Like a poor prisoner in his twisted gyves,[114]
And with a silk thread plucks it back again,
So loving[115] jealous of his[116] liberty.

Romeo   I would I were thy bird.

Juliet   Sweet, so would I.
Yet I should kill thee with much cherishing.[117]
185   Good night, good night. Parting is such sweet sorrow
That I shall say good night till it be morrow.

EXIT

Romeo   Sleep dwell upon thine eyes, peace in thy breast.
Would I were sleep and peace, so sweet[118] to rest.
Hence will I to my ghostly father's[119] close cell,[120]
190   His help to crave[121] and my dear hap[122] to tell.

EXIT

113 wanton's bird = the pet of a playful / spoiled child
114 fetters, shackles, irons
115 (adjective)
116 its
117 pampering, caressing
118 (adverb)
119 spiritual guide / confessor
120 close cell = secluded room, small living quarters
121 request, ask / beg for
122 fortune, luck

SCENE 3
Friar Laurence's cell

ENTER FRIAR, ALONE, WITH A BASKET

Friar [1]The gray-eyed morn smiles on the frowning night,
    Check'ring[2] the eastern clouds with streaks of light,
    And fleckèd[3] darkness like a drunkard reels
    From forth[4] day's path and Titan's fiery wheels.[5]
    Now, ere the sun advance[6] his burning eye   5
    The day to cheer and night's dank[7] dew to dry,
    I must up fill this osier cage[8] of ours
    With baleful weeds[9] and precious juicèd flowers.[10]
    The earth that's nature's mother is her[11] tomb.
    What is her[12] burying grave,[13] that is her[14] womb,   10
    And from her womb children of divers kind
    We[15] sucking on her natural[16] bosom find,
    Many for many virtues[17] excellent,

1 (some texts conclude act 2, scene 2, with the first four lines)
2 marking like a checker- or chessboard
3 dappled, spotted
4 from forth = away from, out of
5 Titan's fiery wheels = the burning wheels of the sun god's chariot
6 move forward, raise, uplift
7 injuriously damp
8 container of woven willow twigs
9 baleful weeds = deadly / destructive / malignant herbs
10 precious juicèd flowers = flowers containing valuable juices
11 nature's
12 nature's
13 place
14 the earth's
15 (the verb of which "we" is the subject is "find")
16 normal, ordinary
17 qualities, properties

None but for some, and yet all different.

15 O mickle[18] is the powerful grace[19] that lies
In plants, herbs, stones, and their true qualities,[20]
For naught so vile[21] that on the earth doth live
But to the earth some special good doth give,
Nor aught so good but, strained[22] from that fair use,
20 Revolts[23] from true birth,[24] stumbling on[25] abuse.
Virtue itself turns[26] vice, being misapplied,
And vice sometime[27] by action dignified.[28]
Within the infant rind[29] of this small flower
Poison hath residence,[30] and medicine power,[31]
25 For this, being smelt, with that part[32] cheers each part,[33]
Being[34] tasted, stays[35] all senses with[36] the heart.
Two such opposèd[37] kings encamp them[38] still

18 much, great
19 wholesome virtue/efficacy
20 capacities, natures
21 wretched, repulsive
22 distorted, pressed, corrupted
23 departs
24 true birth = its correct/real/right/legitimate origin/lineage
25 stumbling on = falling into
26 turns into
27 is sometimes
28 action dignified = what it does is raised/exalted
29 infant rind = new/early stage of the peel/skin/membrane
30 hath residence = is contained
31 medicine power = medical remedies have strength/active capacity
32 quality ("scent")
33 cheers = that quality (its odor) comforts/cures/enlivens everything (all portions)
34 but being
35 stops
36 following on/along with its stopping
37 adverse, hostile
38 encamp them = settle/lodge themselves

In man as well as herbs – grace and rude will[39] –
And where the worser is predominant[40]
Full[41] soon the canker[42] death eats up that plant.   30

ENTER ROMEO

Romeo   Good morrow, father.
Friar   Benedicite![43]
What early[44] tongue so sweet[45] saluteth[46] me?
(*recognizing Romeo*) Young son, it argues[47] a distempered[48]
head
So soon to bid good morrow[49] to thy bed.
Care[50] keeps his watch[51] in every old man's eye,   35
And where care lodges sleep will never lie,
But where unbruisèd[52] youth with unstuffed[53] brain
Doth couch[54] his limbs, there golden sleep doth reign.
Therefore thy earliness doth me assure

39 God's grace and rough/raw human longing/passion (GRACE and rude
   WILL)
40 (the WORser IS preDOMinANT)
41 very
42 ulcerish decay
43 bless you! (BENeDIciTAY)
44 early in the morning
45 (adverb)
46 greets
47 indicates, proves
48 disturbed, troubled
49 morning (greeting it as one leaves it for the new day)
50 sorrow
51 vigilance, wakefulness
52 undamaged (as yet) by life
53 not yet swarming full
54 lie down

40 Thou art uproused with[55] some distemperature.[56]

Or if not so,[57] then here I hit it right —

Our Romeo hath not been in bed tonight.

Romeo That last is true — the sweeter rest was mine.

Friar God pardon sin! Wast thou with Rosaline?

45 *Romeo* With Rosaline, my ghostly father? No.

I have forgot that name, and that name's woe.[58]

Friar That's my good son! But where hast thou been then?[59]

Romeo I'll tell thee ere thou ask it me again.

I have been feasting[60] with mine enemy,

50 Where on a sudden one[61] hath wounded me

That's by me wounded. Both our remedies[62]

Within thy help and holy physic[63] lies.

I bear no hatred, blessèd man, for — lo! —

My intercession[64] likewise steads[65] my foe.

55 *Friar* Be plain, good son, and homely in thy drift.[66]

Riddling[67] confession finds[68] but riddling shrift.

Romeo Then plainly know my heart's dear love is set

---

55 uproused with = awakened by
56 disorder of mind or body (thou ART upROUSED with SOME
    disTEMperTURE)
57 (Romeo perhaps indicates that this is not the case)
58 grief, lamentation
59 (but WHERE hast THOU been THEN)
60 enjoying myself, celebrating, partying
61 someone
62 cures
63 healing knowledge/art
64 my intercession = what I am asking you for
65 profits, helps
66 homely in thy drift = simple/everydaylike in your meaning★
67 puzzling, enigmatic, ambiguous
68 meets with

On the fair daughter of rich Capulet.
As mine on hers, so hers is set on mine,
And all combined,[69] save what thou must combine   60
By holy marriage. When, and where, and how
We met, we wooed and made exchange of vow,
I'll tell thee as we pass.[70] But this I pray,
That thou consent to marry us today.

Friar Holy Saint Francis! What a change is here.   65
Is Rosaline, that thou didst love so dear,
So soon forsaken? Young men's love then lies
Not truly in their hearts, but in their eyes.
Jesu Maria! What a deal of brine[71]
Hath washed thy sallow[72] cheeks for Rosaline.   70
How much salt water thrown away in waste
To season[73] love, that of it doth not taste.
The sun not yet thy sighs from heaven clears,[74]
Thy old groans ring yet in mine ancient ears.
Lo, here upon thy cheek the stain doth sit   75
Of an old tear that is not washed off yet.
If e'er thou wast thyself, and these woes thine,
Thou and these woes were all for Rosaline.
And art thou changed? Pronounce this sentence[75] then:
Women may fall when there's no strength in men.   80

---

69 unified, agreed upon
70 proceed, walk along
71 salt water (tears)
72 sickly yellowish
73 flavor, make savory
74 removes
75 judgment, wise maxim/saying

Romeo Thou chid'st[76] me oft for loving Rosaline.

Friar For doting,[77] not for loving, pupil mine.

Romeo And bad'st me bury love.

Friar   Not in a grave

    To lay one in, another out to have.

85 *Romeo* I pray thee chide not. She whom I love now

    Doth grace[78] for grace and love for love allow.[79]

    The other did not so.

Friar   O she knew well

    Thy love did read by rote,[80] that could not spell.

    But come, young waverer,[81] come go with me.

90   In one respect I'll thy assistant be,

    For this alliance may so happy[82] prove

    To turn your households' rancor to pure love.

Romeo O let us hence! I stand on[83] sudden haste.

Friar Wisely, and slow.[84] They stumble that run fast.

EXEUNT

76 scolded*
77 displaying excessive / foolish / infatuated emotion
78 favor
79 approve of, accept
80 memory
81 shifter back and forth, vacillator
82 lucky, fortunate
83 stand on = insist on
84 wisely, and slow = it is better to proceed wisely and slowly

SCENE 4

A street

ENTER BENVOLIO AND MERCUTIO

Mercutio Where the devil should this Romeo be? Came he not
home tonight?[1]

Benvolio Not to his father's. I spoke with his man.

Mercutio Why, that same pale hard-hearted wench, that
Rosaline, torments him so that he will sure run mad.   5

Benvolio Tybalt, the kinsman to old Capulet, hath sent a letter to
his father's house.

Mercutio A challenge, on my life.

Benvolio Romeo will answer it.

Mercutio Any man that can write may answer a letter.   10

Benvolio Nay, he will answer the letter's master, how[2] he dares,
being dared.

Mercutio Alas, poor Romeo, he is already dead! stabbed with a
white wench's black eye, shot through the ear with a love
song, the very pin[3] of his heart cleft[4] with[5] the blind bow   15
boy's butt shaft[6] – and is he a man to encounter Tybalt?

Benvolio Why, what is Tybalt?

Mercutio More than Prince of Cats.[7] O he's the courageous

---

1 last night
2 how he dares, being dared = saying in what manner/means he undertakes,
  having been challenged
3 peg/nail at the center of a target
4 split
5 by
6 thick arrow used in target shooting
7 (Tibert, in the Old French *Renard the Fox* [trans. Patricia Terry], is "prince"
  of cats as Renard is "prince" of foxes; both the medieval tale and *Romeo and
  Juliet* are brilliantly echoed in S.V. Benét's story "The King of the Cats")

captain[8] of compliments.[9] He fights as you sing pricksong[10]
20   – keeps time, distance, and proportion:[11] rests me his minim
rests,[12] one, two, and the third in your bosom![13] The very
butcher of a silk button,[14] a duelist, a duelist, a gentleman of
the very first house,[15] of the first and second cause.[16] Ah, the
immortal passado,[17] the punto reverso,[18] the hay![19]

25 *Benvolio* The what?

Mercutio The pox of [20] such antic, lisping, affecting
fantasticoes[21] – these new tuners of accent![22] "By Jesu, a very
good blade! a very tall[23] man! a very good whore!" Why, is

8 chief, prince (in modern military usage, a "general")
9 dueling courtesies, Italian style
10 written music, as opposed to that sung from memory or by ear (pricks =
     musical notes set to paper; prick (verb) = to stab, run through)
11 (1) metrical/musical rhythm/harmony, (2) melodic line
12 his minim rests = takes/makes the shortest possible rests/pauses (minim in
     Renaissance musical notation is what is today called a half note)
13 one, two, and the third in your bosom! = (1) then it's one, two, three – and
     all over!, *or* (2) he makes one feint, pauses, then another feint, pauses again,
     and then runs you through!
14 butcher of a silk button = so accurate that he can slice off a button
15 one whose life is governed by the first of the twelve astrological houses, the
     first being the ascendant or most important of all
16 first and second cause = primary reasons for fighting a duel: first, accusation
     of serious crime, second, honor
17 immortal passado = heavenly/famous thrust, sword and one foot moving
     forward at the same time*
18 backhand thrust
19 hay! = Italian *hai* (*avere*, "to have"), "you've got it!" – exclaimed when a
     thrust hits home
20 the pox of = the plague on (in modern English, "damn such . . .")
21 antic, . . . affecting fantasticoes (some texts have "phantasimes") =
     grotesque/bizarre/uncouth/ludicrous . . . full of affectation absurd/
     irrational people
22 tuners of accent! = adjusters of how we speak!
23 active, proper, brave

not this a lamentable thing, grandsir,[24] that we should be thus
afflicted with these strange flies,[25] these fashion mongers,[26]   30
these pardon me's,[27] who stand so much on the new form[28]
that they cannot sit at ease on the old bench?[29] O their
bones, their bones![30]

ENTER ROMEO

Benvolio Here comes Romeo, here comes Romeo!
Mercutio Without his roe,[31] like a dried herring. O flesh, flesh,   35
how art thou fishified![32] Now is he for[33] the numbers[34] that
Petrarch flowed in.[35] Laura,[36] to[37] his lady,[38] was but a
kitchen wench – marry, she had a better love[39] to berhyme
her – [40] Dido a dowdy, Cleopatra a gypsy,[41] Helen and

24 grandfather
25 insignificant insects/flatterers
26 dealers, traffickers
27 people who constantly excuse themselves, in the Continental (very un-English) manner
28 style, model ("form" also = bench)
29 old bench = old style plain/hard wooden seat
30 their bones! = their delicate rear ends aching because of hard wood (there may also be a reference to a link between fashionable men and the "bone ache," as venereal disease was known)
31 without his roe = (1) deprived of his sperm, like a male fish (2) take the letters "r," "o," and "e" out of "Romeo" and you get, more or less, "meo" or "o me," which are typical lovers' cries
32 dried out, after a night of sexual activity
33 ready for
34 poetry, then exclusively metrical (which means "measurement")
35 flowed in = glided along in (see act 1, scene 1, note 47)
36 Petrarch's beloved
37 compared to
38 Romeo's lady, thought by Mercutio to be Rosaline
39 lover
40 Dido, Cleopatra, Helen, Hero, and Thisbe (THIZbee) are all compared to Rosaline; gypsies were believed to have come from Egypt
41 cheating hussies, dark skinned to boot

40   Hero[42] hildings and harlots,[43] Thisbe[44] a gray eye or so,[45] but
            not to the purpose.[46] (*to Romeo*) Signior Romeo, bon jour.
            There's a French salutation to your French slop.[47] You gave
            us the counterfeit fairly[48] last night.

       Romeo   Good morrow to you both. What counterfeit did I give
45   you?

       Mercutio   The slip,[49] sir, the slip. Can you not conceive?[50]

       Romeo   Pardon, good Mercutio. My business was great, and in
            such a case as mine a man may strain[51] courtesy.

       Mercutio   That's as much as to say, such a case as yours constrains a
50   man to bow in the hams.[52]

       Romeo   Meaning, to curtsy.

       Mercutio   Thou hast most kindly[53] hit it.

       Romeo   A most courteous[54] exposition.

       Mercutio   Nay, I am the very pink[55] of courtesy.

55   *Romeo*   Pink for flower.

       Mercutio   Right.

---

42 beloved of Leander (see Christopher Marlowe's "Hero and Leander")
43 hildings and harlots = jades/baggages and whores
44 beloved of Pyramus; they both die
45 a gray eye or so = all of them just females with gray eyes
46 to the purpose = relevant
47 clothing
48 gave us the counterfeit fairly = really/fully deceived us
49 (1) evasion/escape, (2) a counterfeit coin
50 think/imagine it
51 contract, diminish, restrain
52 limits/afflicts a man in bowing the backs of his thighs/knees (your "great
    business" was sexual, and your thighs/knees are weary from it)
53 (1) naturally, characteristically, (2) sympathetically, pleasantly
54 (curtsy-ess)
55 (1) decorative hole punched in clothing/shoes, (2) rapier thrust, (3) flower,
    (4) finest example

Romeo Why, then is my pump[56] well flowered.

Mercutio Sure[57] wit, follow me[58] this jest now till thou hast
worn out thy pump, that,[59] when the single[60] sole of it is
worn,[61] the jest may remain, after the wearing,[62] solely   60
singular.[63]

Romeo O single soled[64] jest, solely singular[65] for the
singleness.[66]

Mercutio Come between us,[67] good Benvolio! My wits faint.[68]

Romeo Swits[69] and spurs,[70] swits and spurs, or I'll cry a match.[71]   65

Mercutio Nay, if our wits run the wild goose chase,[72] I am
done,[73] for thou hast more of the wild goose in one of thy
wits[74] than, I am sure, I have in my whole five. Was I with[75]

56 shoe
57 steadfast
58 me in
59 so that
60 poor, contemptible, thin
61 worn out
62 (1) being used, worn, (2) exhausting, wearing away
63 solely singular = (1) all alone, (2) a singular/unique sole
64 single soled = poor soled/souled
65 solely singular = only unique/superior
66 simplicity, naïveté
67 come between us = help me by stopping these punning exchanges, as
would a second in a duel
68 wits faint = brain gives way/swoons
69 switches, whips
70 use whips and spurs on your faltering mind/steed
71 cry a match = announce/claim that the match is over ("I win!")
72 wild goose chase = a follow the leader race that could lead anywhere, and
was therefore risky
73 finished, used up, worn out
74 faculties, senses (tasting, smelling, hearing, seeing, feeling)
75 alongside, together with/equal to

you there for the goose?[76]

70 *Romeo* Thou wast never with me for anything when thou wast not there for the goose.[77]

Mercutio I will bite thee by the ear[78] for that jest.

Romeo Nay, good goose,[79] bite not![80]

Mercutio Thy wit is a very bitter sweeting,[81] it is a most sharp[82]

75 sauce.[83]

Romeo And is it not, then, well served in to[84] a sweet goose?

Mercutio O here's a wit of cheveril,[85] that stretches from an inch narrow to an ell[86] narrow to an ell broad.

Romeo I stretch it[87] out for that word "broad," which, added to

80 the goose, proves thee far and wide a broad goose.[88]

Mercutio (*happily*) Why, is not this[89] better now than groaning for love? Now art thou sociable, now art thou Romeo, now art thou what thou art, by art[90] as well as by nature. For this driveling love is like a great natural[91] that runs lolling[92] up

---

76 (1) the popular board game, "fox and geese," (2) the eating of the prize goose, after a contest

77 (1) eating the flesh, (2) enjoying the prostitute

78 bite thee by the ear = nibble affectionately on your ear

79 simpleton

80 nay, good goose, bite not = a mock cry: "Oh spare me, terrible creature!"

81 (1) sweetness, sweet flavoring, (2) type of apple often eaten with goose

82 (1) keen, (2) cutting, (3) pungent, caustic

83 (1) sauce, (2) sauciness, impertinence

84 well served in to = properly served with (since sweet dishes go best with pungent sauces)

85 of cheveril = made of kid leather, pliant and easily stretched

86 inches

87 my wit

88 broad goose = plain/obvious/outstanding/vulgar/indecent simpleton

89 this contest of wits

90 skill, learning★

91 half-wit, born fool/idiot

92 lazily

and down to hide his bauble[93] in a hole.[94]   85

Benvolio Stop there, stop there!

Mercutio Thou desirest me to stop[95] in my tale[96] against the
hair.[97]

Benvolio Thou wouldst else have made thy tale large.[98]

Mercutio O thou art deceived! I would have made it short,[99] for   90
I was come to the whole depth[100] of my tale, and meant
indeed to occupy the argument[101] no longer.

Romeo Here's goodly gear![102]

ENTER NURSE AND HER MAN PETER, AT THE OPPOSITE
END OF THE STAGE

Mercutio A sail, a sail![103]

Benvolio Two, two. A shirt and a smock.[104]   95

Nurse Peter.

Peter Anon.

Nurse My fan, Peter.

Mercutio [105]Good Peter, to hide her face, for her fan's the fairer

---

93 toy, worthless/paltry object/thing
94 (1) by burying it, (2) by inserting his thing/penis in a woman's vagina
95 (1) cease, (2) plug, stuff (verb)
96 (1) tale, (2) tail/penis
97 against the hair = (1) contrary to my inclination/its natural direction, (2)
   up against female genital hair
98 tale large = (1) story long, (2) tail/penis large, (3) licentious, improper, gross
99 (1) a short tale, (2) a small tail/penis
100 (1) tale's profundity, sagacity, (2) tail/penis's depth
101 occupy the argument = take possession of the subject/woman
102 here's goodly gear = *either* (1) this kind of talk is first-class stuff, *or* (2) (of
   the Nurse and Peter) here come good toys/stuff/doings
103 the Nurse, a large woman, appears on the horizon like an approaching ship
104 a shirt and a smock = a man and a woman
105 (it is not clear whether this is an aside, to his friends, or is spoken aloud for
   Peter and the Nurse to hear)

100   face[106] of the two.

Nurse   God ye good morrow, gentlemen.

Mercutio   God ye good den, fair gentlewoman.

Nurse   Is it good den?[107]

Mercutio   'Tis no less, I tell ye, for the bawdy[108] hand of the dial is

105   now upon the prick[109] of noon.

Nurse   Out upon you.[110] What[111] a man are you?

Romeo   One, gentlewoman, that God hath made, Himself to
        mar.[112]

Nurse   By my troth,[113] it is well said. "For himself to mar,"

110   quoth[114] 'a? Gentlemen, can any of you tell me where I may
        find the young Romeo?

Romeo   I can tell you, but young Romeo will be older when
        you have found him than he was when you sought him. I am
        the youngest of that name, for fault[115] of a worse.

115 *Nurse*   You say well.

Mercutio   Yea, is the worst well? Very well took,[116] i' faith.
        Wisely, wisely.

Nurse   If you be he, sir, I desire some confidence[117] with you.

Benvolio   She will endite[118] him to some supper.

---

106 (fans often bore painted faces)
107 is it good den? = is it evening?
108 (1) soiled, dirty, (2) lewd, obscene
109 (1) mark on a dial, (2) penis
110 out upon you = (modern usage) come on!
111 what kind of
112 God hath made, Himself to mar = God created man in his image, and man
      spoils that image
113 by my troth = by my faith
114 says
115 lack
116 understood, grasped
117 (1) confidential communication? (2) uneducated mistake for "conference"?
118 deliberate mistake for "invite": Benvolio thinks/wants to think
      "confidence" (see note 117) is an error

Mercutio A bawd, a bawd, a bawd![119] So ho![120]   120

Romeo   (*to Mercutio*) What hast thou found?

Mercutio No hare, sir, unless a hare, sir, in a lenten pie,[121] that is
      something stale and hoar[122] ere it be spent.[123]

HE WALKS BY THEM AND SINGS

     An old hare hoar,[124]
     And an old hare hoar,   125
     Is very good meat in Lent,
     But a hare that is hoar
     Is too much for a score[125]
     When it hoars[126] ere it be spent.[127]

     Romeo, will you come to your father's? We'll to dinner   130
     thither.

Romeo   I will follow you.

Mercutio Farewell, ancient lady. Farewell, (*singing*) "lady, lady,
      lady."[128]

EXEUNT MERCUTIO AND BENVOLIO

119 (1) dialect word for "hare," (2) a procurer/whorehouse proprietor
120 expression used in hunting hares, when a hare is located
121 (in which there should be no meat)
122 something stale and hoar = rather stale and aged (because Lent lasts forty
    days and a hare pie would be long since moldy, if kept – unrefrigerated –
    for any longish period)
123 consumed, used up
124 (1) gray haired, (2) whore (homonym)
125 for a score = (1) excessive, unreasonable, (2) a record of drinks served, in an
    ale house (bar, saloon)
126 ages
127 be spent = (1) is used up/exhausted, (2) results in an orgasm
128 (refrain from "The Ballad of Constant Susanna": "A woman fair and
    virtuous / Lady, lady . . ." See Percy, *Reliques of Ancient English Poetry*,
    1:209–10)

135   *Nurse*   Marry, farewell! I pray you, sir, what saucy merchant[129]
           was this that was so full of his ropery?[130]

      Romeo   A gentleman, Nurse, that loves to hear himself talk and
           will speak more in a minute than he will stand to[131] in a
           month.

140   *Nurse*   An 'a speak anything against me, I'll take him down,[132]
           an 'a were lustier[133] than he is, and twenty such jacks.[134] And
           if I cannot, I'll find those that shall. Scurvy knave![135] I am
           none of his flirt gills,[136] I am none of his skains mates.[137] (*to
           Peter*) And thou must stand by, too, and suffer[138] every knave
145   to use me at his pleasure![139]

      Peter   I saw no man use[140] you at his pleasure. If I had, my
           weapon[141] should quickly have been out, I warrant you. I
           dare draw as soon as another man, if I see occasion[142] in a
           good quarrel,[143] and the law on my side.

150   *Nurse*   Now, afore God, I am so vexed that every part about me
           quivers. Scurvy knave! (*to Romeo*) Pray you, sir, a word, and as

---

129 shopkeeper, tradesman (insulting, when applied to a "gentleman")
130 knavery, tricks
131 stand to = act upon
132 take him down = (1) rebuke, reprimand, (2) humiliate ("take him down a
      peg")
133 (1) stronger, (2) more confident
134 low fellows, knaves
135 scurvy knave = worthless/contemptible/low/badmannered rascal/
      rogue★
136 flirt gills = women of loose/light behavior
137 skains mates = cut-throat companions ("skain" = long Irish knife)
138 allow, tolerate
139 at his pleasure = as he pleases
140 have sexual intercourse with
141 (1) sword, (2) penis
142 (1) favorable circumstances, good reason, (2) pretext, excuse
143 cause, reason

I told you, my young lady bid me enquire you out. What she
bid me say, I will keep to myself, but first let me tell ye, if ye
should lead her into a fool's paradise, as they say, it were a very
gross kind of behavior, as they say; for the gentlewoman is   155
young, and therefore, if you should deal double with her,
truly it were an ill thing to be offered to any gentlewoman,
and very weak dealing.[144]

Romeo Nurse, commend me to thy lady and mistress. I protest
unto thee –   160

Nurse Good heart, and I faith I will tell her as much. Lord,
Lord, she will be a joyful woman.

Romeo What wilt thou tell her, Nurse? Thou dost not mark[145]
me.

Nurse I will tell her, sir, that you do protest,[146] which, as I take 165
it, is a gentlemanlike offer.[147]

Romeo Bid her devise[148]

Some means to come to shrift this afternoon,
And there she shall at Friar Laurence[149] cell
Be shrived[150] and married. Here is[151] for thy pains.   170

Nurse No, truly, sir; not a penny.

Romeo Go to! I say you shall. (she takes the offered gratuity)

Nurse This afternoon, sir? Well, she shall be there.

---

144 weak dealing = feeble, immoral business
145 pay attention to★
146 declare/affirm/vow in solemn terms
147 proposal of marriage
148 plan, think out, contrive★
149 (the original printed texts of the play agree on "Friar Laurence cell."
    Modern editors add an apostrophe after Laurence: Laurence'. This
    preserves the prosody but introduces a form unknown in English)
150 given penance and absolution, after confession
151 is something

Romeo And stay, good Nurse, behind the abbey wall.

175   Within this hour my man shall be with thee

And bring thee cords[152] made like a tackled stair,[153]

Which to the high topgallant[154] of my joy

Must be my convoy[155] in the secret night.

Farewell. Be trusty,[156] and I'll quit[157] thy pains.

180   Farewell. Commend me to thy mistress.

Nurse Now God in heaven bless thee. Hark[158] you, sir.

Romeo What say'st thou, my dear Nurse?

Nurse Is your man secret? Did you ne'er hear say,

Two may keep counsel, putting one away?[159]

185 *Romeo* I warrant thee my man's as true as steel.

Nurse Well, sir, my mistress is the sweetest lady. Lord, Lord!

When 'twas[160] a little prating[161] thing – O there is a

nobleman in town, one Paris, that would fain lay knife

aboard,[162] but she, good soul, had as lief[163] see a toad, a

190   very[164] toad, as see him. I anger her sometimes, and tell her

that Paris is the properer[165] man, but I'll warrant you, when I

152 ropes
153 tackled stair = ladder made of ropes
154 the top of a ship's tallest mast
155 guidance, protection
156 trustworthy, reliable
157 reward, repay
158 listen
159 putting one away = removing/getting rid of/sending away one of the two
160 she was
161 chattering
162 lay knife aboard = set his weapon (sexual allusion) on her
163 as lief = rather
164 honest to God
165 more worthy, better looking

say so, she looks as pale as any clout[166] in the versal[167] world.

Doth not rosemary and Romeo begin both with a letter?

Romeo Ay, Nurse. What of that? Both with an R?

Nurse Ah, mocker! That's the dog's name. R[168] is for the − No,   195
I know. It begins with some other letter, and she hath the
prettiest sententious[169] of it, of you and rosemary, that it
would do you good to hear it.

Romeo Commend me to thy lady.[170]

Nurse Ay, a thousand times.   200

EXIT ROMEO

Peter!

Peter Anon.

Nurse Before, and apace.[171]

EXEUNT

166 scrap of cloth, rag
167 whole, universal
168 sound of a dog growling?
169 aphoristic (terse, proverbial) way of speech
170 (a polite dismissal)
171 before, and apace = go in front of me, and quickly

SCENE 5
Capulet's orchard

ENTER JULIET

Juliet   The clock struck nine when I did send the Nurse;
         In half an hour she promised to return.
         Perchance[1] she cannot meet[2] him. That's not so.
         O she is lame.[3] Love's heralds[4] should be thoughts,
5   Which ten times faster glide than the sun's beams
         Driving back shadows over lowering[5] hills.
         Therefore do nimble-pinioned[6] doves draw Love,[7]
         And therefore hath[8] the wind-swift[9] Cupid wings.
         Now is the sun upon the highmost hill
10   Of this day's journey, and from nine till twelve
         Is three long hours,[10] yet she is not come.
         Had she affections[11] and warm youthful blood
         She would be as swift in motion as a ball.
         My words would bandy[12] her to my sweet love,
15   And his to me.

1 perhaps
2 find
3 infirm, halting, crippled
4 messengers
5 dark, threatening (bisyllabic; the first syllable rhymes with "out" or "ouch")
6 nimble-pinioned = quick/agile/light-winged
7 draw Love = pull the chariot of Venus
8 likewise/also has
9 wind-swift = (compound adjective) swift as wind
10 (bisyllabic: OWerz)(again, rhymes with FLOWerz)
11 feelings, emotions, passions
12 strike, hit (from tennis)★

But old folks, many feign as[13] they were dead –
Unwieldy, slow, heavy and pale as lead.

ENTER NURSE AND PETER

O God, she comes! O honey Nurse, what news?
Hast thou met with him? Send thy man away.
Nurse Peter, stay at the gate.   20

EXIT PETER

Juliet Now, good sweet Nurse – O Lord, why look'st thou sad?
Though news be sad, yet tell them[14] merrily.
If good, thou shamest the music of sweet news
By playing it[15] to me with so sour a face.
Nurse I am aweary, give me leave[16] awhile.   25
Fie, how my bones ache! What a jaunce[17] have I!
Juliet I would thou hadst my bones, and I thy news.
Nay, come, I pray thee speak. Good, good Nurse, speak.
Nurse Jesu, what haste! Can you not stay awhile?
Do you not see that I am out of breath?   30
Juliet How art thou out of breath when thou hast breath
To say to me that thou art out of breath?
The excuse that thou dost make in this delay
Is longer than the tale thou dost excuse.[18]
Is thy news good or bad? Answer to that.   35

13 feign as = act as if they believe themselves, pretend to be
14 ("news" = plural)
15 (the music)
16 give me leave = please leave me alone
17 prancing (like a horse obliged to do tricks)
18 decline/beg off from doing, with apologies/explanations

Say either, and I'll stay the circumstance.[19]

Let me be satisfied: is't good or bad?

Nurse Well, you have made a simple[20] choice. You know not

how to choose a man. Romeo? No, not he. Though his face

40 be better than any man's, yet his leg excels all men's, and for

a hand and a foot, and a body, though they be not[21] to be

talked on, yet they are past compare. He is not the flower of

courtesy, but I'll warrant him as gentle as a lamb. Go thy ways,

wench.[22] Serve God. What, have you dined at home?

45 *Juliet* No, no. But all this did I know before.

What says he of our marriage? What of that?

Nurse Lord, how my head aches! What a head have I!

It beats as[23] it would fall in twenty pieces.

My back o' t' other side – ah, my back, my back!

50 Beshrew[24] your heart for sending me about

To catch my death with jauncing up and down.

Juliet I' faith, I am sorry that thou art not well.

Sweet, sweet, sweet Nurse, tell me, what says my love?

Nurse Your love says, like an honest gentleman, and a courteous,

55 and a kind, and a handsome, and, I warrant, a virtuous –

Where is your mother?

Juliet Where is my mother? Why, she is within.

Where should she be? How oddly thou repliest!

"Your love says, like an honest gentleman,

Where is your mother?"

19 details of time, place, manner, and so on
20 dismal, worthless, stupid
21 not worthy, poor, dismal, silly, foolish
22 girl
23 as if
24 hang, a curse on★

Nurse   O God's Lady dear!   60

    Are you so hot?[25] Marry come up,[26] I trow.[27]

    Is this the poultice for my aching bones?

    Henceforward do your messages yourself.

Juliet. Here's such a coil![28] Come, what says Romeo?

Nurse. Have you got leave[29] to go to shrift to-day?   65

Juliet. I have.

Nurse. Then hie[30] you hence to Friar Laurence cell.

    There stays a husband to make you a wife.

    Now comes the wanton[31] blood up in your cheeks:

    They'll be in scarlet straight[32] at any news.   70

    Hie you to church, I must[33] another way

    To fetch a ladder, by the which your love

    Must climb a bird's nest soon when it is dark.

    I am the drudge, and toil[34] in your delight,

    But you shall bear the burden[35] soon at night.[36]   75

    Go, I'll to dinner. Hie you to the cell.

Juliet Hie to high fortune! Honest Nurse, farewell.

EXEUNT

25 feverish, excited, lustful
26 marry come up = well, hoity toity
27 it seems to me
28 confusion, fuss
29 permission
30 hurry
31 (1) wild, skittish, (2) lascivious, lewd
32 without delay, immediately
33 must go / proceed
34 work hard
35 load: (1) the work, (2) have the weight of a man on you
36 at night = tonight, this night

SCENE 6

Friar Laurence's cell

ENTER FRIAR LAURENCE AND ROMEO

Friar   So smile the heavens upon this holy act
     That afterhours[1] with sorrow chide us not.
Romeo Amen, amen. But come what[2] sorrow can,[3]
     It cannot countervail[4] the exchange of joy[5]
5   That one short minute gives me in her sight.
     Do thou but close[6] our hands with holy words,
     Then love-devouring death do what he dare –
     It is enough I may but call her mine.
Friar   These violent[7] delights have violent ends
10   And in their triumph die, like fire and powder,[8]
     Which, as they kiss, consume. The sweetest honey
     Is loathsome in his own deliciousness
     And in the taste confounds[9] the appetite.
     Therefore love moderately. Long love doth so.
15   Too swift arrives as tardy as too slow.

ENTER JULIET

     Here comes the lady. O, so light a foot
     Will ne'er wear out the everlasting flint.[10]

1 hours yet to come, the future
2 whatever
3 can do
4 match, equal
5 exchange of joy = mutual joy, joy given and received
6 unite, bind (verb)
7 vehement, very strong/intense
8 gunpowder
9 destroys, ruins
10 ground paved with stone

A lover may bestride the gossamer[11]
That idles[12] in the wanton summer air,
And yet not fall, so light[13] is vanity.[14]   20

Juliet   Good even to my ghostly confessor.[15]
Friar   Romeo shall thank thee,[16] daughter, for us both.

ROMEO KISSES HER

Juliet   As much to him,[17] else is his thanks too much.

JULIET KISSES ROMEO

Romeo Ah, Juliet, if the measure[18] of thy joy
Be heaped like mine, and that[19] thy skill be more   25
To blazon[20] it, then sweeten with thy breath[21]
This neighbor[22] air, and let rich music's tongue
Unfold[23] the imagined[24] happiness that both
Receive in either[25] by this dear encounter.[26]

Juliet   Conceit[27] more rich in matter than in words   30

11 filmy spiderwebs
12 lazes (verb)
13 inconsequential, of no importance, of very little weight
14 foolishness, worldly pleasure (which are the same, to Friar Laurence)
15 (CONfesSOR)
16 with a kiss
17 as much to him = I must give as much to him
18 measuring utensil/cup
19 if
20 (1) depict, paint, (2) boast of, proclaim
21 sweeten with thy breath = speak words in
22 nearby, adjoining, surrounding
23 disclose, make clear
24 prospective, future
25 both receive in either = we both of us receive
26 dear encounter = glorious/noble meeting
27 idea, conception★

Brags of his substance,[28] not of ornament.
They are but beggars that[29] can count their worth.
But my true love is[30] grown to such excess
I cannot sum up sum[31] of half my wealth.

35 *Friar* Come, come with me, and we will make short work,
For, by your leaves,[32] you shall not stay[33] alone
Till Holy Church incorporate two in one.

EXEUNT

---

28 his substance = its reality
29 those who
30 has
31 sum up sum = sum up (verb) the sum (noun)
32 by your leaves = with the permission of you both
33 remain, be left

Act 3

SCENE I

A public place

ENTER MERCUTIO, BENVOLIO, AND MEN

Benvolio I pray thee, good Mercutio, let's retire.[1]
  The day is hot, the Capulets abroad,[2]
  And if we meet, we shall not scape[3] a brawl,
  For now, these hot days, is the mad[4] blood stirring.
Mercutio Thou art like one of these fellows that, when he enters   5
  the confines of a tavern, claps me[5] his sword upon the table
  and says "God send me[6] no need of thee!" and by the
  operation[7] of the second cup[8] draws him[9] on the drawer,[10]

1 leave, withdraw
2 are out and about
3 escape
4 mad blood = frenzied, foolish, extravagantly reckless emotions
5 sets/bangs noisily
6 God send me = may God not send me
7 working
8 drink
9 draws him = draws his weapon
10 tapster, bar man

when indeed there is no need.

10 *Benvolio* Am I like such a fellow?

Mercutio Come, come, thou art as hot a jack[11] in thy mood as any in Italy; and as soon moved to be moody,[12] and as soon moody to be moved.

Benvolio And what to?

15 *Mercutio* Nay, an there were two such, we should have none shortly,[13] for one would kill the other. Thou! Why, thou wilt quarrel with a man that hath a hair more or a hair less in his beard than thou hast. Thou wilt quarrel with a man for racking nuts, having no other reason but because thou hast

20 hazel[14] eyes. What eye but such an eye would spy out[15] such a quarrel? Thy head is as full of quarrels as an egg is full of meat,[16] and yet thy head hath been beaten as addle[17] as an egg for quarreling. Thou hast quarreled with a man for coughing in the street, because he hath wakened thy dog that

25 hath lain asleep in the sun. Didst thou not fall out with a tailor for wearing his new doublet[18] before Easter,[19] with another for tying his new shoes with an old riband?[20] And yet thou wilt[21] tutor[22] me from quarreling!

11 man
12 (1) haughty, stubborn, angry, (2) melancholy, sullen
13 speedily, quickly
14 the reddish brown color of a ripe hazelnut
15 spy out = discover, seek out
16 edible matter, food
17 crazy, confused
18 close-fitting body garment, ancestor of modern coats and jackets
19 (the fashion season began at Easter)
20 ribbon
21 want to
22 teach, instruct (verb)

Benvolio An I were so apt[23] to quarrel as thou art, any man
  should buy the fee simple[24] of my life for an hour and a   30
  quarter.[25]

Mercutio The fee simple? O simple![26]

ENTER TYBALT AND OTHERS

Benvolio By my head, here come the Capulets.

Mercutio By my heel,[27] I care not.

Tybalt   (*to other Capulets*) Follow me close, for I will speak to   35
  them.
  Gentlemen, good den. A word with one of you.

Mercutio And but one word with one of us? Couple it with
  something, make it a word and a blow.

Tybalt   You shall find me apt enough to that, sir, an you will
  give me occasion.   40

Mercutio Could you not take some occasion without giving?[28]

Tybalt   Mercutio, thou consortest[29] with Romeo.

Mercutio Consort? What, dost thou make us minstrels?[30] An
  thou make minstrels of us, look to hear nothing but
  discords.[31] (*indicates his sword*) Here's my fiddlestick,[32] here's   45

---

23 ready, prepared, prompt*
24 fee simple = complete and unconditional ownership (usually of land)
25 for an hour and a quarter = for the brief period my life, were I that
   quarrelsome, could be expected to last
26 O simple! = what an awful/pitiful metaphor
27 foot (scornful)
28 without giving = without being given one
29 associate, keep company
30 musicians
31 dissonances, quarrels
32 fiddlestick = violin bow

that[33] shall make you dance. Zounds,[34] consort!

Benvolio We talk here in the public haunt[35] of men.

Either withdraw unto some private place

And reason coldly[36] of your grievances,

50 Or else depart. Here all eyes gaze on us.

Mercutio Men's eyes were made to look, and let them gaze.

I will not budge for no[37] man's pleasure.

ENTER ROMEO

Tybalt Well, peace be with you, sir. Here comes my man.[38]

Mercutio But I'll be hanged,[39] sir, if he wear[40] your livery.

55 Marry, go before to field,[41] he'll be your follower.[42]

Your worship[43] in that sense may call him man.

Tybalt Romeo, the love I bear thee can afford[44]

No better term than this: thou art a villain.

Romeo Tybalt, the reason that I have to love thee

60 Doth much excuse the appertaining[45] rage

To such a greeting. Villain am I none.

Therefore farewell. I see thou knowest me not.

33 that which
34 God's wounds (imprecation)
35 place
36 reason coldly = discuss/converse/argue calmly
37 any
38 (1) the man I'm looking for, (2) servant
39 I'll be hanged = I'll be damned
40 wears
41 go before to field = if you lead the way to the dueling field
42 be your follower = (1) he'll follow you, (2) then he'll be your "servant" (do the courteous thing)
43 your worship = a gentleman/man of high honor like you (sarcastic)
44 supply, furnish (since he in fact feels *no* love for Romeo)
45 proper, appropriate

Tybalt   Boy, this shall not excuse the injuries

    That thou hast done me. Therefore turn and draw.

Romeo   I do protest I never injured thee,   65

    But love thee better than thou canst devise,[46]

    Till thou shalt know the reason of my love.

    And so good Capulet, which name I tender[47]

    As dearly as mine own, be satisfied.

Mercutio O calm, dishonorable, vile submission!   70

    Alla stoccata[48] carries it away. (*he draws*)

    Tybalt, you ratcatcher,[49] will you walk?[50]

Tybalt   What wouldst thou have[51] with me?

Mercutio Good King of Cats, nothing but one of your nine lives.

    That I mean to make bold withal and, as[52] you shall use[53] me   75

    hereafter, dry beat[54] the rest of the eight. Will you pluck[55]

    your sword out of his pilcher[56] by the ears?[57] Make haste, lest

    mine be about[58] your ears ere it be out.

Tybalt   I am for you. (*he draws*)

Romeo   Gentle Mercutio, put thy rapier up.   80

---

46 conceive, imagine
47 cherish, regard
48 *alla stoccata* = fencing thrust: that is, Tybalt (Italian dueling term: *stoccata* = stab, thrust)
49 (as cats are ratcatchers)
50 step aside, withdraw (to fight a duel)
51 do (though Mercutio chooses to understand it, literally, as "have")
52 according to how
53 deal with, behave toward
54 dry beat = beat soundly/severely★
55 pull, snatch (negative usage)
56 scabbard (contemptuous)
57 hilt (which protrudes on either side more or less like ears: a contemptuous metaphor)
58 all around

Mercutio (*to Tybalt*) Come, sir, your *passado*!

THEY FIGHT

Romeo   Draw, Benvolio, beat down their weapons.
Gentlemen, for shame! Forbear⁵⁹ this outrage!⁶⁰
Tybalt, Mercutio! The Prince expressly hath
85   Forbid this bandying in Verona streets.
Hold, Tybalt! Good Mercutio!

TYBALT UNDER ROMEO'S ARM STABS MERCUTIO
AND FLIES WITH HIS FOLLOWERS

Mercutio   I am hurt.
A plague⁶¹ o' both your houses. I am sped.⁶²
Is he gone and hath nothing?
Benvolio   What, art thou hurt?
Mercutio Ay, ay, a scratch, a scratch. Marry, 'tis enough.
90   Where is my page? (*to Page*) Go, villain, fetch a surgeon.⁶³

EXIT PAGE

Romeo   Courage, man. The hurt cannot be much.
Mercutio No, 'tis not so deep as a well, nor so wide as a church
door, but 'tis enough, 'twill serve. Ask for me tomorrow, and
you shall find me a grave man. I am peppered,⁶⁴ I warrant, for
95   this world. A plague o' both your houses. Zounds, a dog, a rat,

59 give up, cease, abstain from
60 rashness, foolhardiness, mad/passionate behavior, insolence
61 curse, divine punishment
62 finished, killed
63 medical man
64 ruined, killed

a mouse, a cat, to scratch[65] a man to death. A braggart, a
rogue, a villain, that fights by the book of arithmetic. Why the
devil came you between us? I was hurt under your arm.

Romeo   I thought all for the best.

Mercutio Help me into some house, Benvolio,   100
Or I shall faint. A plague o' both your houses.
They have made worms' meat of me. I have it,[66]
And soundly too. Your houses!

EXIT, SUPPORTED BY BENVOLIO

Romeo   This gentleman, the Prince's near ally,[67]
My very friend, hath got this mortal hurt   105
In my behalf – my reputation stained
With Tybalt's slander[68] – Tybalt, that an hour[69]
Hath been my kinsman. O sweet Juliet,
Thy beauty hath made me effeminate
And in my temper[70] softened valor's steel.[71]   110

ENTER BENVOLIO

Benvolio O Romeo, Romeo, brave[72] Mercutio's dead,
That gallant[73] spirit hath aspired[74] the clouds,
Which too untimely here did scorn[75] the earth.

65 (1) injure with claws/nails, (2) skirmish, fight without doing serious harm
66 (modern usage: "I've had it")
67 kindred, relation (alLY)
68 insult, malicious defamation/falsehood
69 that an hour = who for one hour
70 (1) character, temperament, (2) the tempering/hardening of steel
71 valor's steel = the toughness of courage/manliness
72 noble, splendid
73 excellent, fine
74 risen/soared/mounted to
75 defied, disdained

Romeo   This day's black fate[76] on moe days[77] doth depend.[78]

115   This[79] but begins the woe others[80] must end.

ENTER TYBALT

Benvolio Here comes the furious[81] Tybalt back again.

Romeo   Alive in triumph, and Mercutio slain?

Away to heaven respective lenity,[82]

And fire-eyed fury be my conduct[83] now!

120   Now, Tybalt, take the "villain" back again

That late thou gavest me, for Mercutio's soul

Is but a little way above our heads,

Staying for thine to keep him company.

Either thou or I, or both, must go with him.

125 *Tybalt*   Thou wretched boy, that didst consort him[84] here,

Shalt with him hence.

Romeo   (*drawing his sword*) This shall determine that.

THEY FIGHT. TYBALT FALLS

Benvolio Romeo, away, be gone.

The citizens are up,[85] and Tybalt slain.

Stand not amazed.[86] The Prince will doom thee[87] death

76 what is destined to happen, destiny
77 moe days = more days, later times
78 doth depend = (1) is contingent upon, (2) will follow from
79 this day
80 other days
81 raging, violent
82 respective lenity = courteous / careful / civil mildness / gentleness
83 guidance
84 with him
85 are up = have risen, are excited / roused
86 bewildered, stunned
87 doom thee = sentence★ you to (verb)

	If thou art taken.[88] Hence, be gone, away!	130
Romeo	O I am fortune's fool.	
Benvolio	Why dost thou stay?	

EXIT ROMEO

ENTER CITIZENS

Citizen   Which way ran he that killed Mercutio?
  Tybalt, that murderer, which way ran he?
Benvolio There lies that Tybalt.
Citizen   Up,[89] sir, go with me.   135
  I charge[90] thee in the Prince's name obey.

ENTER PRINCE, ATTENDED, OLD MONTAGUE, CAPULET,
THEIR WIVES, AND OTHERS

Prince   Where are the vile beginners of this fray?
Benvolio   O noble Prince, I can discover[91] all
  The unlucky manage[92] of this fatal brawl.
  There lies the man, slain by young Romeo,   140
  That slew thy kinsman, brave Mercutio.
Lady Capulet Tybalt, my cousin. O my brother's child!
  O Prince, O husband, O the blood is spilled
  Of my dear kinsman. Prince, as thou art true,
  For blood of ours shed blood of Montague.   145
  O cousin, cousin.
Prince   Benvolio, who began this bloody fray?

---

88 caught, captured, seized★
89 come
90 command
91 make known, disclose
92 actions, conduct

Benvolio Tybalt, here slain, whom Romeo's hand did slay.
Romeo, that spoke him fair,[93] bid him bethink[94]
150 How nice[95] the quarrel was, and urged withal[96]
Your high displeasure.[97] All this – utterèd[98]
With gentle breath, calm look, knees humbly bowed –
Could not take truce[99] with the unruly spleen[100]
Of Tybalt, deaf to peace, but that he tilts[101]
155 With piercing steel at bold Mercutio's breast,
Who, all as hot, turns[102] deadly point to point,
And, with a martial scorn, with one hand beats
Cold death aside and with the other sends
It[103] back to Tybalt, whose dexterity
160 Retorts[104] it. Romeo he cries[105] aloud,
"Hold, friends! Friends, part!" and swifter than his tongue
His agile arm beats down their fatal points
And 'twixt them rushes, underneath whose arm
An envious thrust from Tybalt hit the life
165 Of stout[106] Mercutio, and then Tybalt fled,
But by and by comes back to Romeo,

93 courteously
94 remember
95 foolish, senseless, trivial★
96 in addition, besides
97 high displeasure = exalted / grave anger
98 your HIGH disPLEAsure ALL this UTterED
99 take truce = make peace
100 unruly spleen = disorderly / ungovernable hot / irritable / capricious temper
101 thrusts / strikes at
102 returns, sends back
103 cold death (his own sword point)
104 replies / returns in kind
105 Romeo he cries = Romeo cries
106 proud, brave, formidable

Who had but newly entertained[107] revenge,
And to't[108] they go like lightning, for, ere I
Could draw[109] to part them, was stout Tybalt slain
And as he fell did Romeo turn and fly.[110]   170
This is the truth, or let Benvolio die.

Lady Capulet He is a kinsman to the Montague.
Affection[111] makes him false, he speaks not true.
Some twenty of them fought in this black[112] strife,
And all those twenty could but kill one life.   175
I beg for justice, which thou, Prince, must give.
Romeo slew Tybalt; Romeo must not live.

Prince   Romeo slew him, he slew Mercutio.
Who now the price[113] of his dear[114] blood doth owe?

Montague   Not Romeo, Prince. He was Mercutio's friend.   180
His fault concludes but what the law should end,
The life of Tybalt.

Prince   And for that offense
Immediately we do exile him hence.
I have an interest in your hate's proceeding,
My blood[115] for your rude brawls doth lie ableeding.   185
But I'll amerce[116] you with so strong[117] a fine

107 considered
108 to't (to it) = set to it, attack, fight
109 draw his sword
110 flee
111 (1) kind feeling, (2) bias, partiality
112 foul
113 payment, cost
114 precious
115 my blood = my family's blood, Mercutio being his kinsman
116 punish
117 powerful, massive, severe, heavy

That you shall all repent the loss of mine.
I will be deaf to pleading and excuses;
Nor[118] tears nor prayers shall purchase out[119] abuses.
190   Therefore use none. Let Romeo hence[120] in haste,
Else, when he is found, that hour[121] is his last.
Bear hence[122] this body, and attend[123] our[124] will.
Mercy but murders, pardoning[125] those that kill.

EXEUNT

118 neither
119 purchase out = redeem
120 go away (go hence)
121 (bisyllabic: AWer)
122 away
123 pay heed to
124 my (the royal "we")
125 PARDning

SCENE 2
Capulet's orchard

ENTER JULIET

Juliet Gallop apace,[1] you fiery-footed[2] steeds,
  Towards Phoebus' lodging.[3] Such a wagoner[4]
  As Phaeton[5] would whip you to the west
  And bring in cloudy night immediately.
  Spread thy close[6] curtain, love-performing[7] night,   5
  That runaway[8] eyes may wink,[9] and Romeo
  Leap to these arms untalked of and unseen.
  Lovers can see to do their amorous rites
  By their own beauties, or, if love be blind,
  It best agrees with[10] night. Come, civil[11] night,   10
  Thou sober-suited[12] matron, all in black,
  And learn me how to lose a winning match,[13]
  Played for a pair[14] of stainless[15] maidenhoods.

1 swiftly
2 fiery-footed = glowingly hot-footed (as the horses of Phoebus, the sun god, properly are)
3 dwelling (back to their stable, so it will be night)
4 driver (merry, light tone)
5 (sun god's wild-driving son)
6 (1) secret, (2) snug
7 love-performing (compound adjective)
8 gadding about? night wandering?
9 close
10 best agrees with = is most harmonious with, most favorable to
11 polite, well governed, sober
12 sober-suited = dressed soberly
13 lose a winning match = lose virginity but win (1) a husband/mate, (2) the contest
14 (Juliet and Romeo are both virgins)
15 unblemished, pure

Hood[16] my unmanned[17] blood, bating[18] in my cheeks,

15 With thy black mantle,[19] till strange[20] love, grown bold,[21]

Think true love acted simple modesty.[22]

Come, night. Come, Romeo. Come, thou day in night,[23]

For thou wilt lie upon the wings of night

Whiter than new snow upon a raven's back.

20 Come, gentle night. Come, loving, black-browed night,

Give me my Romeo. And when I shall die[24]

Take him and cut him out in little stars,

And he will make the face of heaven so fine

That all the world will be in love with night

25 And pay no worship to the garish[25] sun.[26]

O I have bought[27] the mansion[28] of a love

But not possessed it, and though I am sold,[29]

Not yet enjoyed. So tedious is this day

16 cover (as young, untrained falcons/hawks are hooded to keep them calm)

17 (1) untrained, not broken in, (2) not subjected to/occupied/possessed by a man

18 fluttering, beating

19 (1) loose, sleeveless cloak, (2) blanket

20 unknown, unfamiliar

21 (1) fearless, (2) without shame

22 think true love acted simple modesty = thinks genuine love performed/represented innocent purity/chastity ("strange love" is the subject of "think")

23 day in night = brightness in darkness

24 (the Elizabethan meaning, sexual climax/orgasm, is plainly most on her mind)

25 gaudy, vulgar, ostentatious

26 ("Take him . . . the garish sun": these four lines make no sense unless Romeo is understood to "die" exactly as Juliet expects to; the verb "take" – which can mean "captivate" as well as "capture," and also has the meaning of "sexually possessing" – then has as its subject the glories that night will bring them)

27 by marriage (both a sacrament *and* a contract)

28 splendid human body (as the mansion "house" inhabited by the soul)

29 I am sold = I, too, as Romeo is, have been sold/acquired in this mutual rite of acquisition

As is the night before some festival
To an impatient child that hath new robes[30]   30
And may not wear them. O here comes my Nurse.

ENTER NURSE, WITH LADDER OF CORDS

And she brings news, and every tongue that speaks
But Romeo's name speaks heavenly eloquence.
Now, Nurse, what news? What hast thou there? The cords
That Romeo bid thee fetch?

Nurse   Ay, ay, the cords.   35

SHE THROWS THEM DOWN

Juliet   Ay me, what news? Why dost thou wring thy hands
Nurse   Ah, weraday![31] He's dead, he's dead, he's dead!
We are undone,[32] lady, we are undone.
Alack the day! He's gone, he's killed, he's dead.
Juliet   Can heaven be so envious?[33]
Nurse   Romeo can,   40
Though heaven cannot. O Romeo, Romeo,
Who ever would have thought it? Romeo!
Juliet   What devil art thou that dost torment me thus?
This torture should be roared in dismal hell.
Hath Romeo slain himself? Say thou but "Ay,"   45
And that bare vowel "Ay" shall poison more
Than the death darting[34] eye of cockatrice.[35]
I am not I, if there be such an "Ay,"

30 clothes
31 welladay, alas★
32 ruined, destroyed
33 spiteful, malicious, full of ill will
34 shooting
35 poisonous monster/serpent that can kill by a glance

Or those eyes[36] shut that make thee answer "Ay."
50   If he be slain, say "Ay," or if not, "no."
Brief[37] sounds determine of[38] my weal[39] or woe.

Nurse I saw the wound, I saw it with mine eyes,
(God save the mark!)[40] here on his manly breast.
A piteous corse,[41] a bloody piteous corse,
55   Pale, pale as ashes, all bedaubed[42] in blood,
All in gore[43] blood. I swounded[44] at the sight.

Juliet O break,[45] my heart. Poor bankrupt, break at once.
To prison, eyes, ne'er look on liberty.
Vile earth,[46] to earth resign,[47] end motion[48] here,
60   And thou and Romeo press[49] one heavy bier.[50]

Nurse O Tybalt, Tybalt, the best friend I had.
O courteous Tybalt. Honest gentleman,
That ever I should live to see thee dead.

Juliet What storm is this that blows so contrary?
65   Is Romeo slaughtered, and is Tybalt dead?
My dear loved cousin, and my dearer lord?

36 those eyes = Romeo's eyes
37 (1) short, (2) hasty, quick★
38 either
39 happiness, success
40 God save the mark! = God help/preserve us!
41 corpse
42 spattered
43 thick, congealing blood (adjective)
44 fainted (swooned)
45 (which can also mean "to ruin financially, to bankrupt")
46 her body
47 to earth resign = to the grave surrender
48 movement (life)
49 weigh down
50 the stand on which coffins are set

Then, dreadful[51] trumpet, sound the general doom,[52]

For who is living, if those two are gone?

Nurse Tybalt is gone, and Romeo banishèd.

Romeo that killed him, he is banishèd.   70

Juliet O God! Did Romeo's hand shed Tybalt's blood?

Nurse It did, it did, alas the day, it did.

Juliet O serpent heart, hid with a flowering face.

Did ever dragon keep[53] so fair a cave?

Beautiful tyrant,[54] fiend angelical,   75

Dove feathered raven, wolvish ravening lamb!

Despisèd substance of divinest show![55]

Just opposite[56] to what thou justly[57] seem'st:

A damnèd saint, an honorable villain!

O nature, what hadst thou to do in hell   80

When thou didst bower[58] the spirit of a fiend

In mortal paradise of such sweet flesh?

Was ever book containing such vile matter

So fairly bound? O that deceit should dwell

In such a gorgeous palace.

Nurse   There's no trust,   85

No faith, no honesty in men, all perjured,

All forsworn,[59] all naught, all dissemblers.

---

51 awe-inspiring
52 general doom = Last Judgment
53 (1) live in, (2) guard
54 desperado, ruffian, villain (in its modern sense)
55 outside appearance
56 just opposite = substance exactly opposite
57 with good reason
58 shelter, enclose
59 liars, breakers of their oaths

Ah, where's my man? Give me some *aqua vitae*.[60]

These griefs, these woes, these sorrows make me old.

Shame come to Romeo.

90 *Juliet*   Blistered be thy tongue

For such a wish. He was not born to shame.

Upon his brow shame is ashamed to sit,

For 'tis a throne where honor may be crowned

Sole monarch of the universal earth.

95   O what a beast was I to chide at him.

Nurse Will you speak well of him that killed your cousin?

Juliet Shall I speak ill of him that is my husband?

Ah, poor my lord,[61] what tongue shall smooth[62] thy name

When I, thy three hours wife, have mangled it?

100   But wherefore, villain, didst thou[63] kill my cousin?

That villain cousin would have killed my husband.

Back, foolish tears, back to your native spring,[64]

Your tributary drops[65] belong to woe,

Which you, mistaking, offer up to joy.

105   My husband lives, that[66] Tybalt would have slain,

And Tybalt's dead, that would have slain my husband.

All this is comfort. Wherefore weep I then?

Some word there was, worser than Tybalt's death,

That murdered me. I would forget it fain,

60 brandy, whiskey (Latin: "water of life")★
61 poor my lord = my poor lord
62 clear, polish
63 Romeo
64 native spring = original/natural place of origin/source
65 tributary drops = drops that pay tribute/swell some larger stream
66 who

But O it presses to[67] my memory   110
Like damnèd guilty deeds to sinners' minds.
"Tybalt is dead, and Romeo – banishèd."
That "banishèd," that one word, "banishèd,"
Hath slain ten thousand Tybalts. Tybalt's death
Was woe enough, if it had ended there,   115
Or if sour woe delights in fellowship[68]
And needly[69] will be ranked[70] with other griefs,
Why followed not, when she said "Tybalt's dead,"
"Thy father," or "thy mother" – nay, or both,
Which modern lamentation might have moved?[71]   120
But with a rearward[72] following Tybalt's death,
"Romeo is banishèd" – to speak that word
Is father, mother, Tybalt, Romeo, Juliet,
All slain, all dead. "Romeo is banishèd":
There is no end, no limit, measure,[73] bound,[74]   125
In that word's death, no words can that woe sound.[75]
Where is my father and my mother, Nurse?
Nurse Weeping and wailing over Tybalt's corse.
Will you go to them? I will bring you thither.
Juliet Wash they his wounds with tears? Mine shall be spent,   130
When theirs are dry, for Romeo's banishment.

67 presses to = forces itself on, attacks/assails/harasses
68 company
69 necessity
70 wishes to be joined/positioned with
71 modern lamentation might have moved = might have provoked/caused
    ordinary lamentation
72 later/subsequent addition (literally: "rearguard")
73 quantity
74 boundary
75 reach to the bottom of

Take up those cords. Poor ropes, you are beguiled,
Both you and I, for Romeo is exiled.[76]
He made you for a highway to my bed,
135 But I, a maid, die maiden widowèd.
Come, cords, come, Nurse. I'll to my wedding bed,
And death, not Romeo, take my maidenhead.

Nurse Hie to your chamber. I'll find Romeo
To comfort you. I wot[77] well where he is.
140 Hark ye, your Romeo will be here at night.
I'll to him. He is hid at Laurence cell.

Juliet O find him! Give this ring to my true knight
And bid him come to take his last farewell.

EXEUNT

76 (exILED)
77 know

SCENE 3
Friar Laurence's cell

ENTER FRIAR LAURENCE

Friar Romeo, come forth, come forth, thou fearful[1] man.
　　Affliction is enamored of thy parts,[2]
　　And thou art wedded to calamity.

ENTER ROMEO

Romeo Father, what news? What is the Prince's doom?
　　What sorrow craves acquaintance at my hand   5
　　That I yet know not?
Friar　　　　　　　　　Too familiar
　　Is my dear son with such sour company.
　　I bring thee tidings of the Prince's doom.
Romeo. What less than doomsday is the Prince's doom?
Friar A gentler judgment vanished[3] from his lips: 10
　　Not body's death, but body's banishment.
Romeo Ha, banishment? Be merciful, say "death,"
　　For exile hath more terror in his look,
　　Much more than death. Do not say "banishment."
Friar Hence from Verona art thou banishèd.   15
　　Be patient, for the world is broad and wide.
Romeo There is no world without[4] Verona walls,
　　But purgatory, torture, hell itself.
　　Hence banishèd is banished from the world,

1 frightened, terrorized
2 personal qualities / attributes★
3 fell (and then disappeared, as spoken words necessarily do)
4 outside

20   And world's exile[5] is death. Then "banishment"

        Is death mis-termed. Calling death "banishment"[6]

        Thou cut'st my head off with a golden axe

        And smilest upon the stroke that murders me.

Friar   O deadly sin, O rude unthankfulness.

25   Thy fault our law calls death, but the kind Prince,

        Taking thy part, hath rushed[7] aside the law

        And turned that black word death to banishment.

        This is dear mercy, and thou see'st it not.

Romeo   'Tis torture, and not mercy. Heaven is here

30   Where Juliet lives, and every cat and dog

        And little mouse, every unworthy[8] thing,

        Live here in heaven and may look on her,

        But Romeo may not. More validity,[9]

        More honorable[10] state,[11] more courtship[12] lives

35   In carrion flies than Romeo. They[13] may seize

        On the white wonder of dear Juliet's hand

        And steal immortal blessing from her lips,

        Who, even in pure and vestal modesty,

        Still blush, as thinking their own kisses sin,

40   But Romeo may not, he is banishèd.

5 (exILE)
6 is DEATH misTERMED. CALLing death BANishMENT
7 forced, driven
8 worthless, undeserving
9 (1) force, strength, effectiveness, (2) value, worth
10 (HONorABle)
11 manner of existence
12 courtliness
13 there are those who ("they" seems not to refer back, as modern pronouns
     tend to do, but forward, to "who blush . . . thinking . . .": can we suspect
     "flies" of existing in "pure and vestal modesty"?)

Flies[14] may do this, but I from this must fly.

They are[15] free men, but I am banishèd.

And sayest thou yet that exile is not death?

Hadst thou no poison mixed, no sharp ground knife,

No sudden mean[16] of death, though ne'er so mean,[17]   45

But "banishèd" to kill me[18] – "banishèd"?

O friar, the damnèd use[19] that word in hell:

Howling attends[20] it. How hast thou the heart,

Being a divine,[21] a ghostly confessor,[22]

A sin absolver, and my friend professed,[23]   50

To mangle me with that word "banishèd"?

Friar Thou fond[24] mad man, hear me a little speak.

Romeo O thou wilt speak again of banishment.

Friar I'll give thee armor to keep off that word,

Adversity's sweet milk, philosophy,   55

To comfort thee, though thou art banishèd.

Romeo Yet "banishèd"? Hang up philosophy.[25]

Unless philosophy can make a Juliet,

Displant[26] a town, reverse a prince's doom,

14 not only men, but even flies
15 are like?
16 means
17 poor, inferior, debased
18 (the syntax is "hadst thou no poison [etc.] . . . to kill me")
19 damnèd use: noun + verb
20 follows, accompanies (in hell)
21 clergyman, priest
22 (CONfesSOR)
23 declared, self-acknowledged, ostensible
24 foolish, silly
25 hang up philosophy = philosophy be hanged
26 substitute for

60   It helps not, it prevails[27] not. Talk no more.

Friar   O then I see that madmen have no ears.

Romeo How should they, when that[28] wise men have no eyes?

Friar   Let me dispute[29] with thee of thy estate.[30]

Romeo Thou canst not speak of that[31] thou dost not feel.

65   Wert thou as young as I, Juliet thy love,

        An hour but married, Tybalt murderèd,

        Doting like me, and like me banishèd,

        Then mightst thou speak, then mightst thou tear thy hair,

        And fall upon the ground, as I do now,

70   Taking the measure[32] of an unmade[33] grave. (*falls at full length*)

KNOCK

Friar   Arise, one knocks. Good Romeo, hide thyself.

Romeo Not I, unless the breath of heartsick groans

        Mist-like[34] enfold me from the search[35] of eyes.

KNOCK

Friar   Hark, how they knock! Who's there? Romeo, arise,

75   Thou wilt be taken. – (*to the person knocking*) Stay awhile! –

        (*to Romeo*) Stand up,

27 succeeds, avails
28 when that = when
29 debate, discuss, argue
30 condition, fortune
31 what
32 taking the measure = measuring
33 not yet made
34 mist-like = like mist
35 scrutiny, examination

KNOCK

run to my study. – (*to the person knocking*) By and by! – (*to Romeo*) God's will,
What simpleness[36] is this. – (*to the person knocking*) I come, I come.

KNOCK

Who knocks so hard? Whence come you? What's your will?
Nurse (*within*) Let me come in, and you shall know my errand.
I come from Lady Juliet.
Friar   Welcome then.   80

ENTER NURSE

Nurse O holy friar, O tell me, holy friar,
Where is my lady's lord, where's Romeo?
Friar There on the ground, with his own tears made drunk.
Nurse O he is even in my mistress' case,
Just in her case. O woeful sympathy,   85
Piteous predicament.[37] Even so lies she,
Blubb'ring and weeping, weeping and blubbering.
Stand up, stand up! Stand, an you be a man.
For Juliet's sake, for her sake, rise and stand!
Why should you fall into so deep an O?[38]   90
Romeo (*rising*) Nurse –
Nurse Ah sir, ah sir, death's the end of all.
Romeo Spak'st thou of Juliet? How is it with her?

36 foolishness
37 state, situation (usually dangerous)
38 so deep an O = so deep a state of lamentation / groaning

Doth not she think me an old[39] murderer,

95   Now[40] I have stained the childhood of our joy
With blood removed[41] but little from her own?
Where is she? And how doth she? And what says[42]
My concealed[43] lady to our canceled love?

Nurse   O she says nothing, sir, but weeps and weeps,
100   And now falls on her bed, and then starts up,
And Tybalt calls, and then on Romeo cries,
And then down falls again.

Romeo   As if that name,[44]
Shot from the deadly level[45] of a gun,
Did murder her, as[46] that name's cursèd hand
105   Murdered her kinsman. O tell me, friar, tell me,
In what vile part of this anatomy
Doth my name lodge?[47] Tell me, that I may sack[48]
The hateful mansion.[49]

HE DRAWS HIS DAGGER

Friar   Hold thy desp'rate hand.
Art thou a man? Thy form cries out thou art,

39 practiced, experienced
40 now that
41 distant in relationship
42 where IS she AND how DOTH she AND what SAYS
43 secret (CONcealed)
44 that name: Romeo
45 aiming
46 just as
47 reside, dwell
48 plunder, despoil
49 (his own body)

Thy tears are womanish, thy wild acts denote[50]   110
The unreasonable[51] fury of a beast.
Unseemly[52] woman in a seeming[53] man,
Or ill beseeming beast in seeming both!
Thou hast amazed me. By my holy order,[54]
I thought thy disposition[55] better tempered.[56]   115
Hast thou slain Tybalt? Wilt thou slay thyself
And slay thy lady, that[57] in thy life lives,
By doing damnèd hate upon thyself?
Why rail'st[58] thou on thy birth, the heaven, and earth,
Since birth and heaven and earth all three do meet   120
In thee at once, which thou at once wouldst lose.[59]
Fie, fie, thou sham'st thy shape,[60] thy love, thy wit,
Which, like a usurer,[61] abound'st in all,[62]
And usest[63] none in that true use[64] indeed
Which should bedeck[65] thy shape, thy love, thy wit.   125

50 indicate
51 irrational
52 unbecoming, indecent
53 a seeming = an apparent
54 by my holy order: an exclamation/oath
55 nature, temperament, inclination
56 better tempered = more elastic, balanced
57 who
58 speak abusively about
59 which thou at once wouldst lose = if you killed/want to kill yourself
60 human and manly
61 a grasping man who lends money at high rates of interest
62 abound'st in all = fairly teems in you (and in all men?)
63 you use (like a usurer, who illicitly – by church doctrine – charges interest
    for the "use" of his money)
64 true use: holy use, as opposed to a usurer's illicit use
65 adorn

Thy noble shape is but a form of wax[66]
Digressing[67] from the valor of a man;
Thy dear love sworn[68] but hollow perjury,[69]
Killing that love which thou hast vowed to cherish;
130   Thy wit, that ornament to shape and love,
Misshapen[70] in the conduct of them both,
Like powder[71] in a skilless soldier's flask,[72]
Is set afire by thine own ignorance
And thou dismembered[73] with thine own defense.[74]
135   What, rouse thee, man! Thy Juliet is alive,
For whose dear sake thou wast but lately[75] dead.
There[76] art thou happy. Tybalt would kill thee,
But thou slew'st Tybalt. There art thou happy too.
The law, that threatened death, becomes thy friend
140   And turns it to exile. There art thou happy.
A pack[77] of blessings light upon thy back;
Happiness courts thee in her best array;[78]
But like a misbehaved and sullen wench
Thou pouts upon thy fortune and thy love.

66 a form of wax = a waxen shape
67 swerving, diverging
68 (adjective modifying "love")
69 hollow perjury = empty falsehod
70 distorted, deformed
71 like powder = as gunpowder
72 gunpowder case, made of horn, leather, or metal
73 ripped apart
74 that which should defend you, in Romeo's case "reason," "intellect"
75 not long since
76 in that / her
77 bundle
78 attire, dress

Take heed, take heed, for such[79] die miserable.   145
Go get thee to thy love, as was decreed,[80]
Ascend her chamber – hence, and comfort her.
But look[81] thou stay[82] not till the watch[83] be set,[84]
For then thou canst not pass[85] to Mantua,
Where thou shalt live till we can find a time   150
To blaze[86] your marriage, reconcile your friends,
Beg pardon of the Prince, and call thee back
With twenty hundred thousand times more joy
Than thou wentst forth in lamentation.[87]
Go before, Nurse. Commend me to thy lady,   155
And bid her hasten all the house to bed,
Which heavy sorrow makes them apt unto.
Romeo is coming.

Nurse   O Lord, I could have stayed here all the night
To hear good counsel. O what learning is.   160
(*to Romeo*) My lord, I'll tell my lady you will come.

Romeo   Do so, and bid my sweet prepare to chide.

NURSE STARTS TO LEAVE, THEN TURNS BACK

Nurse   Here is a ring she bid me give you, sir.
Hie you, make haste, for it grows very late.

EXIT NURSE

79 such people
80 resolved, decided, arranged
81 be careful, make sure
82 linger
83 sentinels, guards ("police")★
84 set in place (for the night), posted
85 get through
86 proclaim and publicize
87 LAmenTAtiON

165 *Romeo* How well my comfort[88] is revived by this.

    Friar   Go hence, good night – and here stands all your state:

        Either be gone before the watch be set,

        Or by the break of day, disguised, from hence.

        Sojourn in Mantua. I'll find out your man,[89]

170   And he shall signify[90] from time to time

        Every good hap[91] to you that chances here.

        Give me thy hand. 'Tis late. Farewell, good night.

   Romeo But that a joy past joy calls out on me,

        It were a grief so brief to part[92] with thee.

175   Farewell.

EXEUNT

---

88 enjoyment, pleasure
89 servant
90 make known
91 good chance/fortune
92 so brief to part = to leave even for such a brief period

SCENE 4
Capulet's house

ENTER OLD CAPULET, LADY CAPULET, AND PARIS

Capulet	Things have fallen out[1], sir, so unluckily

That we have had no time to move[2] our daughter.
Look you, she loved her kinsman Tybalt dearly,
And so did I. Well, we were born to die.
'Tis very late; she'll not come down tonight.   5
I promise you, but for your company,
I would have been abed an hour ago.

Paris   These times of woe afford no times to woo.
Madam, good night. Commend me to your daughter.

Lady Capulet I will, and know[3] her mind early tomorrow.   10
Tonight she's mewed up to[4] her heaviness.

Capulet   Sir Paris, I will make a desp'rate[5] tender[6]
Of my child's love. I think she will be ruled[7]
In all respects by me. Nay more, I doubt it not.
Wife, go you to her ere you go to bed.   15
Acquaint her here of my son[8] Paris' love
And bid her (mark you me?) on Wednesday next –
But, soft. What day is this?

---

1 fallen out = chanced to happen
2 persuade, solicit, propose
3 I will know
4 mewed up to = shut in with her
5 somewhat reckless and unsure
6 offer
7 controlled, guided
8 son-in-law to be, which then meant "son" and was often used in advance of
   actual marriage

Paris   Monday, my lord.

20 *Capulet* Monday! Ha, ha! Well, Wednesday is too soon.

Thursday let it be, a⁹ Thursday, tell her

She shall be married to this noble earl.¹⁰

(*to Paris*) Will you be ready?¹¹ Do you like this haste?

We'll keep¹² no great ado,¹³ a friend or two,

25 For hark you, Tybalt being slain so late,¹⁴

It may be thought we held him¹⁵ carelessly,

Being our kinsman, if we revel much.

Therefore we'll have some half a dozen friends,

And there an end. But what say you to Thursday?

30 *Paris*   My lord, I would that Thursday were tomorrow.

Capulet Well, get you gone. A Thursday be it then.

(*to Lady Capulet*) Go you to Juliet ere you go to bed.

Prepare her, wife, against¹⁶ this wedding day.

(*to Paris*) Farewell, my lord. – (*to Servant*) Light to¹⁷ my

chamber, ho!

35 Afore me.¹⁸ It is so very late that we

May call it early by and by. Good night.

EXEUNT

9 on
10 (that is, "count")
11 willing
12 observe
13 fuss
14 recently, lately
15 held him = esteemed/regarded him
16 with regard to★
17 light to = bring light for my going to
18 (1) (if spoken to a servant): go/walk in front/in advance of me, (2) (if spoken to Paris) O my ("in my very sight/in the presence of God")

SCENE 5

Capulet's orchard

<small>ENTER ROMEO AND JULIET ALOFT, AT THE WINDOW</small>

Juliet   Wilt thou be gone? It is not yet near day.
   It was the nightingale, and not the lark,
   That pierced the fearful[1] hollow of thine ear.
   Nightly she sings on yond pom'granate tree.[2]
   Believe me, love, it was the nightingale.   5
Romeo   It was the lark, the herald of the morn,
   No nightingale. Look, love, what envious streaks
   Do lace[3] the severing[4] clouds in yonder east.
   Night's candles are burnt out, and jocund[5] day
   Stands tiptoe on the misty mountain tops.   10
   I must be gone and live, or stay and die.
Juliet   Yond light is not daylight,[6] I know it, I.
   It is some meteor[7] that the sun exhales
   To be to thee this night a torchbearer[8]
   And light thee on the way to Mantua.   15
   Therefore stay yet, thou need'st not to be gone.
Romeo   Let me be ta'en, let me be put to death.
   I am content, so thou wilt have it so.
   I'll say yon gray is not the morning's eye,

1 apprehensive, full of fear
2 (NIGHTly she SINGS on YOND pomGRANate TREE)
3 embroider, thread
4 separating, parting
5 mirthful, light-hearted
6 (dayLIGHT)
7 flaring light thought to be gaseous vapors from the sun (MEETyor)
8 TORCHbearER

20   'Tis but the pale reflex[9] of Cynthia's brow.[10]

Nor that is not the lark whose notes do beat

The vaulty[11] heaven so high above our heads.

I have more care[12] to stay than will to go.

Come, death, and welcome. Juliet wills it so.

25   How is't, my soul?[13] Let's talk, it is not day.

Juliet   It is, it is. Hie hence, be gone, away.

It is the lark that sings so out of tune,

Straining[14] harsh discords[15] and unpleasing sharps.[16]

Some say the lark makes sweet division.[17]

30   This[18] doth not so, for she divideth us.

Some say the lark and loathèd toad change[19] eyes.

O now I would they had changed voices too,

Since arm from arm[20] that voice doth us affray,[21]

Hunting thee hence with "Hunt's up"[22] to the day.

35   O now be gone, more light and light it grows.

Romeo   More light and light, more dark and dark our woes.

ENTER NURSE

9 reflection
10 Cynthia's brow = the moon's forehead
11 arched like a vault
12 concern, solicitude, desire
13 my soul = Juliet
14 constricting its throat to produce, forcing
15 dissonances
16 shrill, high-pitched notes
17 melody, song (diVISiON)
18 this particular lark
19 exchanged (toads having large and lovely eyes, larks small and uninteresting eyes)
20 arm from arm = each other's arms
21 disturb, frighten
22 (song calling sleepers to wake and join the hunt)

Nurse Madam.

Juliet Nurse?

Nurse Your lady mother is coming to your chamber.

The day is broke, be wary, look about.   40

EXIT

Juliet Then, window, let day in, and let life out.

Romeo Farewell, farewell. One kiss, and I'll descend.[23]

HE GOES DOWN

Juliet Art thou gone so, love[24] lord, ay husband friend?[25]

I must hear from thee every day in the hour,

For in a minute there are many days.   45

O by this count I shall be much in years

Ere I again behold my Romeo.

Romeo Farewell.

I will omit no opportunity

That may convey my greetings, love, to thee.   50

Juliet O think'st thou we shall ever meet again?

Romeo I doubt it not, and all these woes shall serve

For sweet discourses[26] in our time to come.

Juliet O God, I have an ill-divining[27] soul!

Methinks I see thee, now thou art below,   55

As one dead in the bottom of a tomb.

23 (using his rope ladder)
24 (some texts follow "love" with a comma)
25 love lord = compound noun; husband friend = compound noun, though
    friend = lover (texts vary a great deal)
26 conversations
27 ill-divining = foreseeing evil (compound adjective)

Either my eyesight fails, or thou look'st pale.

Romeo And trust me, love, in my eye so do you.

Dry[28] sorrow drinks our blood. Adieu, adieu.

EXIT

60 *Juliet*   O Fortune, Fortune! All men call thee fickle.

If thou art fickle, what dost thou with him

That is renowned for faith? Be fickle,[29] Fortune,[30]

For then I hope thou wilt not keep him long

But send him back.

Lady Capulet (*within*) Ho, daughter. Are you up?

65 *Juliet*   Who is't that calls? It is my lady mother.

Is she not down[31] so late, or up so early?

What unaccustomed cause procures[32] her hither?

ENTER LADY CAPULET

Lady Capulet Why, how now, Juliet?

Juliet   Madam, I am not well.

Lady Capulet Evermore weeping for your cousin's death?

70 What, wilt thou wash him from his grave with tears?

An if thou couldst,[33] thou couldst not make him live.

Therefore have done. Some[34] grief shows much of love,[35]

But much of grief shows still some want[36] of wit.

28 thirsty
29 fickle with him
30 Fortuna, a goddess
31 gone to bed
32 induces, brings, urges
33 wash him from his grave
34 a certain amount of
35 much of love = much love
36 (noun)

Juliet   Yet let me weep for such a feeling[37] loss.

Lady Capulet So shall you feel the loss, but not the friend[38]   75
   Which you weep for.

Juliet   Feeling so the loss,
   I cannot choose but ever weep the friend.[39]

Lady Capulet Well, girl, thou weep'st not so much for his death
   As that the villain lives which slaughtered him.

Juliet   What villain, madam?

Lady Capulet   That same villain Romeo.   80

Juliet   (*aside*) Villain and he be many miles asunder.[40]
   (*to Lady Capulet*) God pardon him: I do, with all my heart,
   And yet no man like[41] he doth grieve my heart.

Lady Capulet That is because the traitor murderer lives.

Juliet   Ay, madam, from the reach of these my hands.   85
   Would none but I might venge my cousin's death.

Lady Capulet We will have vengeance for it, fear thou not.
   Then weep no more. I'll send to one[42] in Mantua,
   Where that same banished runagate[43] doth live,
   Shall give him such an unaccustomed dram[44]   90
   That he shall soon keep Tybalt company;
   And then I hope thou wilt be satisfied.

Juliet   Indeed I never shall be satisfied[45]
   With Romeo till I behold him – dead –

37 emotional, heartfelt (adjective)
38 "friend" also means "lover" (though Lady Capulet does not so intend it)
39 friend = lover (and Juliet does so intend it)
40 separated, apart
41 in the same way, as much as
42 someone, some person
43 runaway, fugitive
44 unaccustomed dram = strange potion/drink★
45 sexually satisfied (which Lady Capulet did not mean to say)

95   Is my poor heart[46] so[47] for a kinsman vexed.[48]

       Madam, if you could find out but a man

       To bear a poison, I would temper[49] it,

       That[50] Romeo should, upon receipt[51] thereof,

       Soon sleep[52] in quiet.[53] O how my heart abhors

100   To hear him named and cannot[54] come to him,[55]

       To wreak[56] the love I bore my cousin Tybalt

       Upon his body[57] that[58] hath slaughtered him.

  Lady Capulet Find thou the means, and I'll find such a man.

       But now I'll tell thee joyful tidings, girl.

105 *Juliet*   And joy comes well in such a needy time.

       What are they, I beseech your ladyship?

46 Lady Capulet hears "till I behold [Romeo] dead." But Juliet, who is deceiving her mother all through the scene, means "till I behold [Romeo], dead is my poor heart . . ." Pausing before and after "dead" is the key.

47 thus, in that way

48 a kinsman vexed = a relative (as Romeo is to her, by marriage, though Lady Capulet does not know Juliet is married) troubled / harassed / grieved (as Romeo certainly is and as Tybalt can no longer be, since he is past all feeling)

49 (1) mix, add to (which Lady Capulet understands), (2) make it suitable / proper, reduce / modify / moderate (which Juliet in fact means)

50 so that

51 (1) ingesting (which Lady Capulet understands), (2) receiving (which Juliet means)

52 (1) die (as Lady Capulet understands), (2) sleep (as Juliet means)

53 in quiet = (1) lifeless (which Lady Capulet understands), (2) peacefully (as Juliet means)

54 and cannot = when I cannot

55 come to him = (1) get at him (which Lady Capulet understands), (2) be with him (as Juliet means)

56 (1) force (which Lady Capulet understands), (2) press (which Juliet means)

57 upon his body (1) against his body (which Lady Capulet understands), (2) with his body – that is, sexually (as Juliet means)

58 he who

Lady Capulet Well, well, thou hast a careful[59] father, child,
   One who, to put thee from[60] thy heaviness,
   Hath sorted out[61] a sudden[62] day of joy
   That thou expects not nor I looked not for.   110
Juliet   Madam, in happy time.[63] What day is that?
Lady Capulet Marry,[64] my child, early next Thursday morn
   The gallant, young, and noble gentleman,
   The County Paris, at Saint Peter's Church,
   Shall happily make thee there a joyful bride.   115
Juliet   Now by Saint Peter's Church, and Peter[65] too,
   He shall not make me there a joyful bride.
   I wonder at[66] this haste, that I must wed
   Ere he[67] that should[68] be husband[69] comes to woo.
   I pray you tell my lord and father, madam,   120
   I will not marry yet, and when I do, I swear[70]
   It shall be Romeo, whom you know I hate,
   Rather than Paris. These are news indeed.
Lady Capulet Here comes your father. Tell him so yourself,
   And see how be will take it at your hands.   125

   59 considerate, solicitous
   60 put thee from = remove / divert you from★
   61 sorted out = ordained, ordered, arranged
   62 (1) unexpected, (2) speedy
   63 in happy time = excellent! very good!
   64 (an exclamation, not a verb: originally an ejaculatory evocation of the
      Virgin Mary, but by Shakespeare's time virtually devoid of its original
      significance)
   65 by Saint Peter
   66 wonder at = am surprised by
   67 the man
   68 ought to, must
   69 my husband
   70 (a hexameter line)

ACT 3 • SCENE 5

ENTER CAPULET AND NURSE

Capulet   When the sun sets the air doth drizzle dew,[71]
        But for the sunset[72] of my brother's son
        It rains downright.[73]
        How now? A conduit,[74] girl? What, still in tears?
130   Evermore showering? In one little body
        Thou counterfeit'st[75] a bark,[76] a sea, a wind:
        For still thy eyes, which I may call the sea,
        Do ebb and flow with tears; the bark thy body is,
        Sailing in this salt flood; the winds, thy sighs,[77]
135   Who raging[78] with thy tears, and they with them,[79]
        Without[80] a sudden calm will overset[81]
        Thy tempest-tossèd[82] body. How now, wife?
        Have you delivered[83] to her our decree?[84]
Lady Capulet Ay, sir, but she will none,[85] she gives you thanks.
140   I would the fool were married to her grave.
    Capulet   Soft. Take me with you,[86] take me with you, wife.

71 doth drizzle dew: as if weeping for the departure of the sun
72 death
73 coming down perpendicularly, out and out
74 fountain, water pipe
75 imitate, simulate
76 small-sized sailing vessel
77 the winds, thy sighs = the winds are (in Capulet's metaphor) your sighs
78 which, if they (the winds) behave wildly / violently
79 and they with them = and vice versa
80 unless there is
81 overthrow, overcome, capsize
82 hurled, disordered
83 (1) given, (2) spoken
84 decision
85 will none = wants no part of it ("wishes not at all")
86 take me with you = let me understand you

How? Will she none? Doth she not give us thanks?
Is she not proud?[87] Doth she not count her[88] blest,
Unworthy[89] as she is, that we have wrought[90]
So worthy a gentleman to be her bridegroom? 145

Juliet　　Not proud[91] you have, but thankful[92] that you have.
Proud[93] can I never be of what I hate,[94]
But thankful even for hate[95] that is meant[96] love.

Capulet　How, how, how, how, chop logic?[97] What is this?
"Proud," and "I thank you," and "I thank you not," 150
And yet "not proud"? Mistress minion[98] you,
Thank me no thankings, nor proud me no prouds,
But fettle[99] your fine joints[100] 'gainst[101] Thursday next
To go with Paris to Saint Peter's Church,
Or I will drag thee on a hurdle[102] thither. 155
Out, you green sickness[103] carrion![104] Out, you baggage![105]

---

87 honored, gratified, pleased
88 herself
89 undeserving
90 produced
91 pleased
92 grateful
93 pleased
94 of what I hate = by what I am averse to
95 aversion
96 meant to be
97 hair splitter, sophist (some texts have "chopped logic")
98 hussy, over-dainty
99 prepare, make ready
100 fine joints = perfect/elegant/delicate body ("bones")★
101 toward, in preparation for ("against")
102 wooden sledge (on which criminals were conveyed to their place of execution)
103 green sickness = adolescent, immature (compound adjective)
104 carcass (nothing more than worthless flesh)
105 (1) rubbish, trash, dirt, (2) slut, whore

You tallow[106] face!

Lady Capulet (to Capulet) Fie, fie. What, are you mad?

Juliet   Good father, I beseech you on my knees,
          Hear me with patience but to speak a word.

SHE KNEELS

160 Capulet   Hang thee, young baggage, disobedient wretch!
          I tell thee what. Get thee to church a[107] Thursday
          Or never after look me in the face.
          Speak not, reply not, do not answer me.
          My fingers itch. Wife, we scarce[108] thought us blest
165   That God had lent us but this only child,
          But now I see this one is one too much,
          And that we have a curse in having her.
          Out on her, hilding.[109]

Nurse   God in heaven bless her.
          You are to blame,[110] my lord, to rate[111] her so.

170 Capulet   And why, my Lady Wisdom? Hold your tongue,
          Good Prudence. Smatter[112] with your gossips, go.

Nurse   I speak no treason.

Capulet   O God i' god en![113]

Nurse   May not one speak?

---

106 wax (adjective)
107 on
108 barely, hardly ("scarcely")
109 wretch, jade, baggage
110 wrong ("to be blamed")
111 scold / reprove angrily
112 chatter, prate
113 God 'i god en = for God's sake ("may God give her a good evening" – that is, get rid of her)

Capulet	Peace, you mumbling fool!

Utter your gravity[114] o'er a gossip's bowl,[115]

For here we need it not.

Lady Capulet	You are too hot.	175

Capulet   God's bread,[116] it makes me mad. Day, night, late, early,

At home, abroad, alone, in company,

Waking or sleeping, still my care[117] hath been

To have her matched.[118] And having now provided

A gentleman of princely parentage,   180

Of fair demesnes,[119] youthful, and nobly trained,[120]

Stuffed, as they say, with honorable parts,

Proportioned[121] as one's thought would wish a man –

And then to have a wretched puling[122] fool,

A whining mammet,[123] in her fortune's tender,[124]   185

To answer "I'll not wed, I cannot love,

I am too young, I pray you pardon me"!

But, an you will not wed, I'll pardon you.

Graze[125] where you will, you shall not house[126] with me.

114 grave/serious/weighty remarks
115 drinking vessel
116 God's bread = consecrated wafer (an oath)
117 attention, concern
118 married
119 possessions, estates (dehMEENZ)
120 educated
121 composed (physically)
122 whining, wailing
123 doll, puppet
124 in her fortune's tender = when good fortune is offered to her
125 feed, pasture
126 dwell (verb)

190   Look to't, think on't, I do not use to[127] jest.

Thursday is near, lay hand on heart,[128] advise.[129]

An you be mine,[130] I'll give you to my friend—

An you be not, hang![131] Beg! Starve! Die in the streets!

For, by my soul, I'll ne'er acknowledge[132] thee,

195   Nor what[133] is mine shall never do thee good.

Trust to't. Bethink you. I'll not be forsworn.[134]

EXIT

Juliet   Is there no pity sitting in the clouds

That sees into the bottom of my grief?

O sweet my mother, cast me not away.

200   Delay this marriage for a month, a week,

Or if you do not, make the bridal bed

In that dim monument where Tybalt lies.

Lady Capulet   Talk not to me, for I'll not speak a word.

Do as thou wilt, for I have done with thee.

EXIT

205 *Juliet*   O God! O Nurse, how shall this be prevented?

My husband is on earth, my faith in heaven.

How shall that faith return again to earth

---

127 do not use to = am not in the habit of
128 lay hand on heart = think seriously/carefully/deeply
129 consider (verb)
130 an you be mine = if you are truly/really my daughter
131 go to the devil ("go and be hanged – so you can go where you belong, to hell")
132 show any recognition/acknowledgment of
133 what property/funds
134 be forsworn = obliged to break my word

Unless that husband send it me[135] from heaven
By leaving earth?[136] Comfort me, counsel me.
Alack, alack, that heaven should practice stratagems[137]   210
Upon so soft[138] a subject[139] as myself.
What say'st thou? Hast thou not a word of joy?
Some comfort, Nurse.

Nurse   Faith, here it is.
Romeo is banished, and all the world to nothing[140]
That he dares ne'er come back to challenge[141] you,   215
Or if he do, it needs must be by stealth.
Then, since the case so stands as now it doth,
I think it best you married with the County.
O he's a lovely gentleman.
Romeo's a dishclout[142] to him. An eagle, madam,   220
Hath not so green,[143] so quick, so fair an eye
As Paris hath. Beshrew my very heart,
I think you are happy in this second match,
For it excels your first, or if it did not,
Your first is dead – or 'twere as good he were   225
As living here and you no use of[144] him.

Juliet   Speak'st thou this from thy heart?

Nurse   And from my soul too, else beshrew them both.

135 to me
136 leaving earth = dying
137 practice stratagems = play tricks, work schemes
138 quiet, mild, docile
139 person
140 all the world to nothing = the chances are a million to one
141 find fault with, accuse
142 dish cloth
143 (hazel-green eyes were considered handsome)
144 use of = profit from (especially sexual profit)

Juliet Amen.

230 *Nurse* What?

Juliet Well, thou hast comforted me marvelous much.

Go in, and tell my lady I am gone,

Having displeased my father, to Laurence cell,

To make confession and to be absolved.

235 *Nurse* Marry, I will, and this is wisely done.

EXIT

Juliet Ancient damnation![145] O most wicked fiend,

Is it more sin to wish me thus forsworn,[146]

Or to dispraise my lord with that same tongue

Which she hath praised him with[147] above compare[148]

240 So many thousand times? Go, counselor.

Thou and my bosom henceforth shall be twain.[149]

I'll[150] to the friar to know his remedy.[151]

If all else fail, myself have power to die.

EXIT

145 ancient damnation! = damned old devil!
146 perjured
147 which she hath praised him with = with which she has praised him
148 above compare = beyond comparison
149 parted, separated, estranged
150 I'll go
151 help, relief★

Act 4

SCENE I
Friar Laurence's cell

ENTER FRIAR LAURENCE AND COUNTY PARIS

Friar On Thursday, sir? The time is very short.
Paris My father Capulet will have it so,
　　And I am nothing slow[1] to slack[2] his haste.
Friar You say you do not know the lady's mind.
　　Uneven[3] is the course.[4] I like it not.　　　　　　　　5
Paris Immoderately she weeps for Tybalt's death,
　　And therefore have I little talked of love,
　　For Venus smiles not in a house[5] of tears.
　　Now sir, her father counts it dangerous[6]

---

1 I am nothing slow = I myself am not at all / in no way inclined
2 to slack = making less active / vigorous
3 irregular
4 path
5 (not a human place of dwelling but an astrological position)
6 hurtful, injurious

10   That she do give her sorrow so much sway,[7]
        And in his wisdom hastes[8] our marriage[9]
        To stop the inundation[10] of her tears,
        Which, too much minded[11] by herself alone,[12]
        May be put from her by society.[13]
15   Now do you know the reason of this haste.
    Friar (*aside*) I would I knew not why it should[14] be slowed. –
        Look, sir, here comes the lady toward my cell.

                    ENTER JULIET

    Paris Happily met, my lady and my wife.
    Juliet That may be, sir, when I may be a wife.
20 *Paris* That may be must be, love, on Thursday next.
    Juliet What must be shall be.
    Friar   That's a certain[15] text.
    Paris Come you to make confession to this father?
    Juliet To answer that, I should confess to you.
    Paris Do not deny to him that you love me.
25 *Juliet* I will confess to you that I love him.
    Paris So will ye,[16] I am sure, that you love me.
    Juliet If I do so, it will be of more price,[17]

    7 influence, power of command
    8 (verb)
    9 (MAriAGE)
    10 overflowing, flooding, superfluous abundance
    11 thought of, focused on
    12 when alone
    13 companionship
    14 ought
    15 fixed, settled
    16 so will ye = so too will you confess to him
    17 value, worth

Being spoke behind your back, than to your face.

Paris Poor soul, thy face is much abused[18] with tears.

Juliet The tears have got small victory by that,   30

For it was bad enough before their spite.[19]

Paris Thou wrong'st it more than tears with that report.[20]

Juliet That is no slander, sir, which is a truth,

And what I spake, I spake it to my face.[21]

Paris Thy face is mine, and thou hast slandered it.   35

Juliet It may be so, for it is not mine own.[22]

Are you at leisure, holy father, now,

Or shall I come to you at evening mass?

Friar My leisure serves me,[23] pensive[24] daughter, now.

(*to Paris*) My lord, we must entreat[25] the time alone.   40

Paris God shield[26] I should disturb[27] devotion.

Juliet, on Thursday early will I rouse ye.

Till then, adieu, and keep this holy kiss.

EXIT

Juliet O, shut the door, and when thou hast done so

Come weep with me — past hope, past cure, past help!   45

Friar Ah, Juliet, I already know thy grief.

18 misused, worn out
19 injury, harm
20 statement
21 (pun on saying thing's to a person's face and, here, literally saying it to a face — her face)
22 (that is, it belongs to the man who is already her husband, Romeo)
23 serves me = is my servant/helper ("obeys me")
24 (1) thoughtful, serious, (2) anxious, apprehensive
25 ask for
26 prevent
27 trouble, interfere with

It strains[28] me past the compass[29] of my wits.
I hear thou must — and nothing may prorogue[30] it —
On Thursday next be married to this County.

50 *Juliet* Tell me not, friar, that thou hear'st of this,
Unless thou tell me how I may prevent it.
If in thy wisdom thou canst give no help,
Do thou but call my resolution[31] wise
And with this knife I'll help[32] it presently.[33]

55 God joined my heart and Romeo's, thou[34] our hands,
And ere this hand, by thee to Romeo's sealed,[35]
Shall be the label[36] to another deed,[37]
Or my true heart with treacherous revolt[38]
Turn to another, this shall slay them both.[39]

60 Therefore, out of thy long experienced time,[40]
Give me some present[41] counsel, or behold,
'Twixt my extremes[42] and me this bloody knife
Shall play the umpire, arbitrating[43] that

28 distresses, afflicts, presses hard upon
29 limits, bounds
30 delay, postpone
31 solution, answer
32 do what is needed, bring it to pass
33 speedily, without delay, right now★
34 you joined
35 fastened, tied
36 ribbon to which a documentary seal is attached
37 (1) action, (2) written document of a legal nature
38 rebellion
39 hand and heart
40 years, life
41 quick, immediate, instant★
42 'twixt my extremes = between my utterly opposed/harsh/severe/
   intolerable circumstances
43 deciding, determining

Which[44] the commission[45] of thy years and art
Could to no issue[46] of true honor bring.   65
Be not so long to speak. I long to die
If what thou speak'st speak not of remedy.
Friar Hold, daughter. I do spy a kind of hope,
Which craves as desperate an execution[47]
As that is desperate which we would prevent.   70
If, rather than to marry County Paris
Thou hast the strength of will to slay thyself,
Then is it likely thou wilt undertake
A thing like death to chide[48] away this shame,
That cop'st[49] with death himself to scape from it.   75
And if thou dar'st, I'll give thee remedy.
Juliet O bid me leap, rather than marry Paris,
From off the battlements[50] of yonder tower,
Or walk in thievish ways,[51] or bid me lurk[52]
Where serpents are. Chain me with roaring bears,   80
Or shut me nightly in a charnel house,[53]
O'ercovered quite[54] with dead men's rattling bones,

44 that which = what
45 authority
46 end, termination, way out, exit
47 carrying into effect, fulfillment (which CRAVES as DESprit an EXeCUtiON)
48 drive
49 (1) barters, bargains, (2) encounters, faces
50 tops of the walls
51 thievish ways = (1) dishonest paths, (2) paths/roads where thieves congregate
52 live, hide
53 charnel house = funeral parlor
54 completely

With reeky shanks[55] and yellow chapless[56] skulls,
Or bid me go into a new-made grave
85 And hide me with a dead man in his shroud —
Things that, to hear[57] them told, have made me tremble —
And I will do it without fear or doubt,
To live an unstained[58] wife to my sweet love.
Friar Hold,[59] then. Go home, be merry, give consent
90 To marry Paris. Wednesday is tomorrow.
Tomorrow night look that thou lie alone.
Let not the Nurse lie with thee in thy chamber.
Take thou this vial,[60] being then[61] in bed,
And this distilling[62] liquor drink thou off,
95 When presently through all thy veins shall run
A cold and drowsy humor,[63] for no pulse
Shall keep his native progress,[64] but surcease,[65]
No warmth, no breath, shall testify thou livest,
The roses in thy lips and cheeks shall fade
100 To wanny ashes,[66] thy eyes' windows[67] fall

55 reeky shanks = blackened leg bones
56 jawless
57 to hear = even/just to hear
58 spotless, pure, unblemished, untarnished
59 continue, stay as you are, carry on
60 small glass bottle
61 being then = when you are
62 concentrated, purified
63 state of being ("humors" concerned both matters physiological *and* psychological)
64 native progress = natural march/onward movement
65 stop
66 wanny ashes = pale as ashes (some texts have "wany," or "paly," or "many," or "mealy")
67 eyes' windows = eyelids

Like death when he shuts up[68] the day[69] of life.

Each part, deprived of supple government,[70]

Shall stiff and stark[71] and cold appear, like death,

And in this borrowed likeness of shrunk[72] death

Thou shalt continue two and forty hours   105

And then awake as from a pleasant sleep.

Now when the bridegroom in the morning comes

To rouse thee from thy bed, there art thou dead.

Then as the manner of our country is,

In thy best robes, uncovered on the bier,   110

Thou shalt be borne to that same ancient vault[73]

Where all the kindred of the Capulets lie.

In the meantime, against thou shalt awake,

Shall Romeo by my letters know our drift,

And hither shall he come, and he and I   115

Will watch thy waking, and that very night

Shall Romeo bear thee hence to Mantua.

And this shall free thee from this present shame,

If no inconstant toy[74] nor womanish fear

Abate[75] thy valor in the acting it.   120

Juliet Give me,[76] give me! O tell not me of fear.

---

68 shuts up = closes
69 light ("daylight")
70 supple government = control/management of the flexibility of body and
   limbs
71 hard, rigid
72 contracted, shrunken
73 burial chamber
74 inconstant toy = fickle/changeable whim/foolish fancy
75 (1) destroy, demolish, (2) beat back, diminish, reduce
76 give me = give it to me

Friar Hold. Get you gone, be strong and prosperous[77]
    In this resolve.[78] I'll send a friar with speed
    To Mantua, with my letters to thy lord.
125 *Juliet* Love give me strength, and strength shall help afford.[79]
    Farewell, dear father.

EXEUNT

77 successful
78 (1) decision, solution, (2) firmness of purpose
79 help afford = afford (give, furnish) help

SCENE 2
Capulet's house

ENTER CAPULET, LADY CAPULET, NURSE,
AND TWO OR THREE SERVINGMEN

Capulet   (*to Servingman*) So many guests invite as here are
writ.

EXIT SERVINGMAN

Sirrah, go hire me twenty cunning[1] cooks.

Servingman 2 You shall have none ill,[2] sir, for I'll try[3] if they can
lick their fingers.   5

Capulet   How canst thou try them so?

Servingman 2 Marry, sir, 'tis an ill cook that cannot lick his own
fingers.[4] Therefore he that cannot lick his fingers goes not[5]
with me.

Capulet   Go, begone.[6]   10

EXIT SERVINGMAN 2

We shall be much unfurnished[7] for this time.

What, is my daughter gone to Friar Laurence?

Nurse   Ay, forsooth.

Capulet Well, he may chance to do some good on[8] her.

---

1 skillful, expert
2 of inferior quality
3 test
4 (because a bad cook knows the food does not taste good)
5 goes not = (1) does not travel/join, (2) won't be successful
6 leave
7 unprepared
8 to

15   A peevish[9] self willed harlotry[10] it is.

ENTER JULIET

Nurse   See where she comes from shrift with merry look.

Capulet How now, my headstrong?[11] Where have you been
       gadding?[12]

Juliet   Where I have learnt me to repent the sin
       Of disobedient opposition[13]

20   To you and your behests,[14] and am enjoined[15]
       By holy Laurence to fall prostrate here
       To beg your pardon. (*she kneels*) Pardon, I beseech you.
       Henceforward I am ever ruled by you.

Capulet Send for the County. Go tell him of this.

25   I'll have this knot[16] knit up tomorrow morning.

Juliet   I met the youthful lord at Laurence cell
       And gave him what becoming love[17] I might,
       Not stepping o'er the bounds of modesty.

Capulet Why, I am glad on't. This is well. Stand up.

30   This is as't should be. Let me see the County.
       Ay, marry, go, I say, and fetch him hither.
       Now, afore God, this reverend holy friar,
       All our whole city is much bound[18] to him.

---

9 silly, foolish
10 obscene behavior/talk
11 willful/stubborn one
12 wandering
13 (of DISoBEEDyent OPoSItiON)
14 commands
15 directed, instructed
16 union, tie ("marriage")
17 becoming love = suitable/proper reverence/affection
18 obliged, grateful

Juliet	Nurse, will you go with me into my closet
	To help me sort[19] such needful ornaments[20] 35
	As you think fit to furnish me[21] tomorrow?
Lady Capulet	No, not till Thursday. There is time enough.
Capulet	Go, Nurse, go with her. We'll to church tomorrow.

EXEUNT JULIET AND NURSE

Lady Capulet	We shall be short in our provision.[22]
	'Tis now near night.
Capulet	Tush, I will stir about,[23] 40
	And all things shall be well, I warrant thee, wife.
	Go thou to Juliet, help to deck up[24] her.
	I'll not to bed tonight, let me alone.
	I'll play the housewife for this once. (*calls for servants*) What, ho!
	(*to Lady Capulet*) They are all forth.[25] Well, I will walk myself 45
	To County Paris, to prepare him up
	Against[26] tomorrow. My heart is wondrous light,
	Since this same wayward[27] girl is so reclaimed.[28]

EXEUNT

19 choose, decide on
20 attire, trappings (clothing of a decorative nature)
21 furnish me = provide for myself
22 household arrangements / supplies
23 stir about = busy myself
24 deck up = clothe / adorn / outfit
25 out, away
26 prepare him up against = ready him for
27 disobedient, wrongheaded, self-willed, stubborn
28 brought / called back, reformed

SCENE 3
Juliet's chamber

ENTER JULIET AND NURSE

Juliet   Ay, those attires[1] are best. But, gentle Nurse,
I pray thee leave me to myself tonight,
For I have need of many orisons[2]
To move the heavens to smile upon my state,[3]
5   Which, well thou knowest, is cross[4] and full of sin.

ENTER LADY CAPULET

Lady Capulet What, are you busy, ho? Need you my help?
Juliet   No, madam. We have culled[5] such necessaries
As are behoveful[6] for our state tomorrow.
So please you, let me now be left alone,
10   And let the Nurse this night sit up with you,
For I am sure you have your hands full all[7]
In this so sudden business.
Lady Capulet   Good night.
Get thee to bed, and rest, for thou hast need.

EXEUNT MOTHER AND NURSE

Juliet   Farewell. God knows when we shall meet again.

1 dresses
2 prayers
3 condition (state of mind)
4 unfavorable
5 chosen, gathered, picked★
6 useful, proper
7 (1) all = completely, (2) all of you ("you all have your hands full")

I have a faint[8] cold fear thrills[9] through my veins   15
That almost freezes up the heat of life.
I'll call them back again to comfort me.
Nurse! – What should she do here?
My dismal scene[10] I needs must act alone.
Come, vial.   20
What if this mixture do not work at all?
Shall I be married then tomorrow morning?
No, no! This shall forbid[11] it. (*speaks to her dagger*) Lie thou
there.

LAYS DAGGER DOWN

What if it be a poison which the friar
Subtly[12] hath ministered[13] to have me dead,   25
Lest in this marriage he should be dishonored
Because he married me before to Romeo?
I fear it is. And yet methinks it should not,[14]
For he hath still been tried[15] a holy man.
I will not entertain[16] so bad a thought.   30
How if, when I am laid into the tomb,
I wake before the time that Romeo
Come to redeem[17] me? There's a fearful point.

---

8 (1) sickly, (2) cowardly
9 trickling
10 dismal scene = sinister/terrible/miserable activity/episode
11 stop it, make it impossible
12 (1) cleverly, artfully, (2) treacherously
13 furnished, supplied
14 should not = should not be
15 still been tried = always been proven
16 admit, consider
17 free, recover

Shall I not then be stifled in the vault,

35 To whose foul mouth no healthsome air breathes in,

And there die strangled ere my Romeo comes?

Or, if I live, is it not very like[18]

The horrible conceit of death and night,

Together with the terror of the place,

40 As in[19] a vault, an ancient receptacle[20]

Where for this many hundred years the bones

Of all my buried ancestors are packed[21] –

Where bloody Tybalt, yet but green in earth,[22]

Lies fest'ring[23] in his shroud – where, as they say,

45 At some hours in the night spirits resort.[24]

Alack, alack, is it not like that I,

So early waking, what with loathsome smells,

And shrieks like mandrakes[25] torn out of the earth,

That living mortals, hearing them, run mad –

50 O if I wake, shall I not be distraught,

Environèd with[26] all these hideous fears,

And madly play with my forefathers' joints,[27]

And pluck[28] the mangled[29] Tybalt from his shroud,

18 likely, probable
19 as in = since I will be in
20 repository
21 pressed together in a mass, stuffed, crammed
22 green in earth = newly buried
23 rotting
24 come
25 mandragora: a split-rooted, humanlike plant that was thought, when pulled up, to give a maddening shriek
26 environèd with = beset by
27 (MY foreFATHer's JOINTS)
28 pull, remove, drag
29 mutilated

And, in this rage,[30] with some great kinsman's bone
As with a club dash out my desp'rate brains?   55
O look, methinks I see my cousin's ghost
Seeking out Romeo, that[31] did spit[32] his body
Upon a rapier's point. Stay, Tybalt, stay!
Romeo, Romeo, Romeo, here's drink! I drink to thee.[33]

SHE DRINKS AND FALLS UPON HER BED

30 madness, fit
31 who
32 thrust through, pierce (to out on a spit)
33 (ROmeo ROmeo ROmeo here's DRINK i DRINK to THEE)

SCENE 4

Capulet's house

ENTER LADY CAPULET AND NURSE

Lady Capulet Hold,[1] take these keys and fetch more spices,
Nurse.

Nurse   They call for dates and quinces in the pastry.[2]

ENTER CAPULET

Capulet   Come, stir, stir, stir![3] The second cock hath
crowed,

The curfew bell hath rung, 'tis three o'clock.

5   Look to the baked meats,[4] good Angelica.[5]

Spare not[6] for cost.

Nurse   Go, you cot queen,[7] go,

Get you to bed. Faith, you'll be sick tomorrow

For[8] this night's watching.

Capulet   No, not a whit.[9] What, I have watched ere now

10   All night for lesser cause,[10] and ne'er been sick.

Lady Capulet Ay, you have been a mouse hunt[11] in your time,

---

1 here
2 in the pastry kitchen (possibly, but less likely, in the pastries themselves)
3 move, keep busy
4 baked meats = meat pies ("pastries")
5 the Nurse's name
6 spare not = don't hold back
7 cot queen = a man meddling in women's business
8 on account/because of
9 least little bit
10 motive, reason, purpose
11 mouse hunt = night prowler (like a cat, a hunter of mice; a woman, in slang,
   was a "mouse")

But I will watch you from[12] such watching now.

EXEUNT LADY CAPULET AND NURSE

Capulet   A jealous hood,[13] a jealous hood!

ENTER THREE OR FOUR SERVINGMEN, WITH SPITS,[14]
LOGS, AND BASKETS

Now, fellow, what is there?

Servingman 1 Things for the cook, sir, but I know not what.   15

Capulet   Make haste, make haste.

EXIT SERVINGMAN 1

(*to Servingman 2*) Sirrah,
fetch drier logs.

Call Peter, he will show thee where they are.

Servingman 2 I have a head, sir, that will find out logs

And never trouble Peter for[15] the matter.

Capulet   Mass,[16] and well said. A merry whoreson,[17] ha.   20
Thou shalt be loggerhead.[18]

EXIT SERVINGMAN 2

Good faith, 'tis day.
The County will be here with music,[19] straight,

12 watch you from = be alert/on guard to keep you from
13 (exact meaning uncertain, but the general sense seems clear: "you're jealous of my former exploits!")
14 sharp rods, metal or wood, to be pierced through meat for roasting over a fire
15 about
16 by the Mass (exclamation)
17 slangy praise ("a merry s.o.b.")
18 blockhead: a bad pun on "using his head" and being the "head" of the hunt for "logs"
19 musicians

For so he said he would.

MUSIC

I hear him near.

Nurse! Wife! What, ho! What, Nurse, I say![20]

ENTER NURSE

25   Go waken Juliet, go and trim[21] her up.
I'll go and chat with Paris. Hie, make haste,
Make haste! The bridegroom he is come already:
Make haste, I say.

EXEUNT

20 (NURSE WIFE what HO what NURSE i SAY)
21 (1) dress, (2) support, comfort, (3) strengthen, (4) get ready

SCENE 5
Juliet's chamber

ENTER NURSE

Nurse Mistress! What, mistress! Juliet! Fast,[1] I warrant her, she.
   Why, lamb, why, lady! Fie, you slug-abed!
   Why, love, I say! Madam! Sweetheart! Why, bride!
   What, not a word? You take your pennyworths[2] now.
   Sleep for a week – for[3] the next night, I warrant,   5
   The County Paris hath set up his rest[4]
   That you shall rest but little. God forgive me![5]
   Marry, and amen. How sound is she asleep!
   I needs must wake her. Madam, madam, madam!
   Ay, let the County take you[6] in your bed,   10
   He'll fright you up, i' faith. Will it not be?[7]

SHE DRAWS BED CURTAINS ASIDE

   What, dressed, and in your clothes, and down[8] again?
   I must needs wake you. Lady! Lady! Lady!
   Alas, alas! Help, help! My lady's dead!
   O weraday that ever I was born!   15

---

1 fast asleep
2 small bits of sleep
3 because
4 set up his rest = resolved/determined (based on usages from card playing)
5 (for her bawdiness)
6 take you = catch/find (with the added meaning of "take" as sexual possession)
7 will it not be? = (1) isn't that the way it will be? *or* (2) won't you ever wake up?
8 lying down

Some *aqua vitae,* ho! My lord! My lady!

ENTER LADY CAPULET

Lady Capulet What noise[9] is here?
Nurse   O lamentable[10] day!
Lady Capulet What is the matter?
Nurse   Look, look! O heavy[11] day!
Lady Capulet O me, O me! My child, my only life!
20   Revive,[12] look up,[13] or I will die with thee!
        Help, help! Call help!

ENTER CAPULET

Capulet   For shame, bring Juliet forth, her lord is come.
Nurse   She's dead, deceased.[14] She's dead! Alack the day!
Lady Capulet Alack the day, she's dead, she's dead, she's dead!
25 *Capulet*   Ha! let me see her. Out alas.[15] She's cold,
        Her blood is settled[16] and her joints are stiff.
        Life and these lips have long been separated.
        Death lies on her like an untimely frost
        Upon the sweetest flower of all the field.
    Nurse   O lamentable day!
30 *Lady Capulet*   O woeful time!
    Capulet   Death, that hath ta'en her hence to make me wail,

9 shouting, loud cries
10 (LAmenTAble)
11 grievous, distressful
12 (1) return to consciousness, (2) return to life
13 look up = open your eyes
14 (not then an uncommon word in ordinary vocabularies, "deceased" carried
    the sense of "recently" dead)
15 out alas = exclamation of lamentation
16 stagnant, coagulated, not flowing

Ties up my tongue and will not let me speak.

ENTER FRIAR LAURENCE AND THE COUNTY PARIS,
WITH MUSICIANS

Friar	Come, is the bride ready to go to church?
Capulet	Ready to go, but never to return.

(*to Paris*) O son, the night before thy wedding day 35
Hath Death[17] lain with thy wife. See, there she lies,
Flower as she was, deflowered[18] by him.
Death is my son in law, Death is my heir.
My daughter he hath wedded. I will die
And leave him all. Life – living – all is Death's. 40

Paris Have I thought long to see[19] this morning's face,[20]
And doth it give me[21] such a sight as this?

Lady Capulet Accursed, unhappy, wretched, hateful day!
Most miserable hour that e'er time saw
In lasting labor[22] of his pilgrimage![23] 45
But one, poor one, one poor and loving child,
But one thing to rejoice and solace in,
And cruel Death hath catched[24] it from my sight!

Nurse O woe! O woeful, woeful, woeful day!
Most lamentable day, most woeful day 50

---

17 Death: masculine, in English (though feminine in most European languages)
18 her virginity taken
19 thought long = yearned, waited wearily/impatiently
20 morning's face = dawn
21 give me = bestow on me, put before me
22 lasting labor = enduring/permanent/long-continuing work/task/exertion
23 long journey
24 driven, chased

That ever, ever I did yet behold!

O day, O day, O day! O hateful day!

Never was seen so black a day as this.

O woeful day! O woeful day.

55 *Paris*   Beguiled,[25] divorcèd,[26] wrongèd, spited,[27] slain.[28]

Most detestable[29] Death, by thee beguiled,

By cruel,[30] cruel thee quite overthrown.[31]

O love! O life not life, but love in death!

Capulet Despised,[32] distressèd,[33] hated, martyred, killed.

60 Uncomfortable[34] time, why cam'st thou now

To murder,[35] murder our solemnity?[36]

O child, O child! My soul, and not my child,

Dead art thou. Alack, my child is dead,

And with my child my joys are burièd.

65 *Friar*   Peace, ho, for shame! Confusion's cure[37] lives not

In these confusions.[38] Heaven and yourself

Had part[39] in this fair maid. Now heaven hath all,

And all the better is it for the maid.

25 deceived, cheated

26 a marriage cut/broken off

27 treated maliciously

28 slaughtered

29 (DEEtesTABle)

30 (bisyllabic)

31 vanquished

32 unvalued, treated with contempt/scorn

33 afflicted, exhausted, crushed

34 unconsoling, empty of comfort (unCOMforTAble)

35 kill with premeditated/deliberate malice

36 specially important/observed ritual occasion

37 confusion's cure = the remedy for destruction/ruin

38 agitated/fluttering disorderly displays

39 a share (parents create the body; God creates – and then takes back – the soul)

Your part in her you could not keep from death,
But heaven keeps his part in eternal life.   70
The most you sought was her promotion,[40]
For 'twas your heaven[41] she should be advanced –
And weep ye now, seeing she is advanced
Above the clouds, as high as heaven itself?
O in this[42] love, you love your child so ill[43]   75
That you run mad, seeing that she is well.[44]
She's not well married that lives married long,
But she's best married that dies married young.[45]
Dry up your tears and stick your rosemary[46]
On this fair corse, and, as the custom is,   80
In all her best array bear her to church.
For though fond[47] nature bids us all lament,
Yet nature's tears are reason's[48] merriment.

Capulet All things that we ordainèd[49] festival
Turn from their office[50] to black funeral,   85
Our instruments[51] to melancholy bells,[52]

---

40 elevation/advance/progression to a higher rank (from "maid" to "wife")
   (proMOtiON)
41 (their heaven, but not God's, the only true heaven)
42 this kind of
43 wrongfully, sinfully, wickedly
44 fortunate, happy (with a pun on "well" as "not sick in body")
45 (again, Juliet is considered already married to Paris: the wedding solemnizes
   the prior fact)
46 evergreen leaves, signifying remembrance (ROSEmaRY)
47 insipidly/foolishly tender/loving
48 reason = the ordered/logical/reasonable/believable teaching of religion
49 prepared, arranged, made ready
50 duty, employment, obligation*
51 (of celebratory music making)
52 (funeral church bells)

Our wedding cheer[53] to a sad burial feast,

Our solemn hymns[54] to sullen[55] dirges[56] change,

Our bridal flowers serve for a buried corse,

90   And all things change them[57] to the contrary.

Friar   Sir, go you in, and madam, go with him,

And go, Sir Paris. Everyone prepare

To follow this fair corse unto her grave.

The heavens do low'r[58] upon you for some ill:[59]

95   Move them no more by crossing[60] their high will.

EXEUNT ALL BUT MUSICIANS AND NURSE

Musician 1   Faith, we may put up our pipes and be gone.

Nurse   Honest good fellows, ah, put up, put up!

For well you know this is a pitiful case.[61]

EXIT NURSE

Musician 1   Ay, by my troth, the case[62] may be amended.[63]

ENTER PETER

100 Peter   Musicians, O, musicians, "Heart's ease,"[64] "Heart's

---

53 mirth, joy
54 (in praise)
55 gloomy, dismal, melancholy
56 (prayers / rituals in memoriam)
57 themselves
58 frown, scowl (spelled "lour" or "lower")
59 morally wrong action / conduct
60 thwarting, opposing
61 situation
62 the case in which his musical instrument is carried
63 improved, repaired
64 popular song, the words to which are lost; an earlier poem, "Death the Port of Peace," supplies the customary message: "Here is the rest of all your

ease"! O an you will have me live, play "Heart's ease."

Musician 1 Why "Heart's ease"?

Peter O, musicians, because my heart itself plays "My heart
is full of woe." O, play me some merry dump[65] to comfort
me.   105

Musician 1 Not a dump we! 'Tis no time to play now.

Peter You will not then?

Musician 1 No.

Peter I will then give it you soundly.[66]

Musician 1 What will you give us?   110

Peter No money, on my faith, but the gleek.[67] I will give
you the minstrel.[68]

Musician 1 Then will I give you the serving creature.

Peter Then will I lay[69] the serving creature's dagger on
your pate.[70] I will carry no crotchets.[71] I'll *re*[72] you, I'll *fa*   115
you. Do you note[73] me?

Musician 1 An you *re* us and *fa* us, you note us.[74]

Musician 2 Pray you put up your dagger, and put out[75] your wit.

---

busyness, / Here is the port of peace and restfulness" (normalized from
Religious Lyrics of the Fifteenth Century, ed. Carleton Brown [Oxford: Oxford
University Press, 1939], 259)

65 tune, melody
66 thoroughly, properly, to the full (with a pun on "soundly" as by means of
   "sounds")
67 jest, mockery
68 buffoon, clown
69 bring/beat down, deposit, apply
70 head
71 carry no crotchets = endure no (1) perverse/cranky whims, (2) musical
   notes (as one "carries" a tune)
72 (*do, re, me, fa, so* = Italian words for the notes of the musical scale)
73 (1) mark, pay attention to, (2) set musical notes to words, (3) play music
74 note us = (1) put musical notes on us, (2) pay close attention to us
75 put/give forth, utter, show

Peter Then have at you with my wit. I will dry beat you
120 with an iron wit, and put up[76] my iron dagger. Answer me
like men:

   "When griping[77] grief the heart doth wound,
   And doleful dumps[78] the mind oppress,
   Then music with her silver sound" — [79]

125 Why "silver sound"? Why "music with her silver sound"?
What say you, Simon Catling?[80]

Musician 1 Marry, sir, because silver hath a sweet sound.

Peter Pretty.[81] What say you, Hugh Rebeck?[82]

Musician 2 I say "silver sound" because musicians sound[83] for
130 silver.

Peter Pretty too. What say you, James Soundpost?[84]

Musician 3 Faith, I know not what to say.

Peter O I cry you mercy.[85] You are the singer.[86] I will say[87]
for you. It is "music with her silver sound" because musicians
135 have no gold for sounding:[88]

---

76 put up = sheathe
77 painful, distressing
78 low / heavy spirits, fits of melancholy / depression
79 Richard Edwards (1523?–1566), "A Song to the Lute in Musicke," in Percy,
 Reliques of Ancient English Poetry, 1:187–89
80 catling = cat gut for the strings of musical instruments
81 clever, ingenious
82 early form of the fiddle
83 make sounds, play music
84 wooden peg beneath the bridge of violins, etc., connecting the instrument's
 back and belly
85 I cry you mercy = I beg your pardon (here ironic)
86 (all you can do is sing / play music)
87 speak (which you as a "singer" plainly cannot be expected to do)
88 jingling in their purses

"Then music with her silver sound
With speedy help doth lend redress."

EXIT PETER

Musician 1   What a pestilent[89] knave is this same.[90]
Musician 2   Hang him, Jack. Come, we'll in here, tarry[91] for the
mourners, and stay[92] dinner.   140

EXEUNT

89 annoying, troublesome
90 same/identical man
91 delay, linger, wait for
92 stay to

Act 5

SCENE I
Mantua. A street

ENTER ROMEO

Romeo If I may trust the flattering[1] truth of sleep
My dreams presage[2] some joyful news at hand.[3]
My bosom's lord[4] sits lightly[5] in his throne,[6]
And all this day an unaccustomed[7] spirit

5   Lifts me above the ground with cheerful thoughts.
I dreamt my lady came and found me dead –
Strange dream that gives a dead man leave[8] to think! –
And breathed[9] such life with kisses in my lips

---

1 promising, pleasing
2 predict / foreshadow (by supernatural means)
3 at hand = near, close by
4 bosom's lord = love
5 easily, cheerfully
6 his heart
7 unaccustomed spirit = unusual / strange / unfamiliar emotion / feeling
8 permission
9 breathed into me

That I revived and was an emperor.
Ah me, how sweet is love itself[10] possessed,   10
When but love's shadows[11] are so rich in joy.

ENTER BALTHASAR, ROMEO'S MAN, WEARING RIDING BOOTS

News from Verona! How now, Balthasar?[12]
Dost thou not bring me letters from the friar?
How doth my lady? Is my father well?
How fares my Juliet?[13] That I ask again,   15
For nothing can be ill if she be well.
Balthasar Then she is well, and nothing can be ill.
Her body sleeps in Capel's monument,[14]
And her immortal part with angels lives.[15]
I saw her laid low[16] in her kindred's vault   20
And presently took post[17] to tell it you.
O pardon me for bringing these ill news,
Since you did leave it for my office, sir.
Romeo   Is it e'en[18] so? Then I defy[19] you, stars![20]
(*to Balthasar*) Thou knowest my lodging. Get me ink and
paper   25

10 in and of itself
11 paler/fainter images/traces
12 (BALthaSAR)
13 (JULyet)
14 sepulcher, tomb
15 (verb)
16 under the ground
17 took post = hurried, by means of hiring horses to be available at stages in his
   journey
18 really, truly, indeed
19 repudiate, challenge★
20 astrologically determined fate

And hire posthorses.[21] I will hence[22] tonight.

Balthasar I do beseech you, sir, have patience.[23]

Your looks are pale and wild and do import[24]

Some misadventure.[25]

Romeo   Tush, thou art deceived.

30   Leave me and do the thing I bid thee do.

Hast thou no letters to me from the friar?

Balthasar No, my good lord.

Romeo   No matter. Get thee gone

And hire those horses. I'll be with thee straight.

EXIT BALTHASAR

Well, Juliet, I will lie with thee tonight.

35   Let's see for means. O mischief,[26] thou art swift

To enter in the thoughts of desperate men.

I do remember an apothecary,[27]

And hereabouts 'a dwells, which[28] late I noted

In tattered weeds,[29] with overwhelming[30] brows,

40   Culling of simples.[31] Meager[32] were his looks,

---

21 (see note 17, just above)
22 leave
23 have patience = be calm/move slowly
24 indicate, predict
25 bad luck/fortune
26 evil, misfortune, calamity
27 dealer in/maker of drugs
28 who
29 clothes
30 overhanging, jutting (because lack of food has caused his eyes to seem sunken?)
31 simples = herbs/leaves/roots
32 lean, emaciated

Sharp[33] misery had worn him to the bones,
And in his needy[34] shop a tortoise hung,
An alligator stuffed, and other skins
Of ill-shaped fishes, and about his shelves
A beggarly account[35] of empty boxes,   45
Green earthen[36] pots, bladders,[37] and musty[38] seeds,
Remnants of packthread,[39] and old cakes of roses[40]
Were thinly[41] scattered to make up a show.[42]
Noting this penury,[43] to myself I said,
"An if a man did need a poison now,   50
Whose sale is present death in Mantua,
Here lives a caitiff[44] wretch would sell it him."[45]
O this same thought did but forerun[46] my need,
And this same needy man must[47] sell it me.
As I remember, this should be the house.   55
Being holiday, the beggar's shop is shut.
What, ho! Apothecary!

33 keen, piercing, severe
34 poor
35 beggarly account = poverty-stricken number/sum/amount
36 clay
37 taken from dead animals and used, much like plastic bags, as containers
      (especially of liquids)
38 moldy
39 twine, cord
40 cakes of roses = compacted rose petals, used for their scent
41 sparsely
42 make up a show = produce/represent/constitute the appearance of a
      mercantile display
43 extreme poverty
44 miserable, piteous (from "captive")
45 to him
46 anticipate
47 (1) could, (2) should (is likely to), (3) needs/is obliged to

ENTER APOTHECARY

Apothecary	Who calls so loud?
Romeo	Come hither, man. I see that thou art poor.

        Hold, there is forty ducats.[48] Let me have

60   A dram of poison, such[49] soon-speeding gear[50]

        As will disperse[51] itself through all the veins

        That the life-weary[52] taker may fall dead,

        And that[53] the trunk[54] may be discharged[55] of breath

        As violently as hasty[56] powder fired

65   Doth hurry from the fatal[57] cannon's womb.

Apothecary Such mortal[58] drugs I have, but Mantua's law

        Is death to any he[59] that utters[60] them.

Romeo   Art thou so bare[61] and full of wretchedness

        And fearest to die? Famine is in thy cheeks,

70   Need and oppression[62] starveth[63] in thine eyes,

        Contempt[64] and beggary hangs upon thy back.

---

48 gold coins
49 such a
50 soon speeding gear = quick-moving (1) stuff, (2) corrupt/foul matter
51 distribute, circulate, spread
52 life-weary = (compound adjective)
53 and that = so that
54 body
55 freed, emptied, relieved
56 rapid, speedy
57 fateful, ruinous, deadly
58 deadly, destructive
59 person
60 sells
61 deprived, poverty-stricken, destitute
62 misfortune, distress
63 suffer most intensely, wither
64 dishonor, disgrace

The world is not thy friend, nor the world's law.

The world affords[65] no law to make thee rich.

Then be not poor, but break it[66] and take this.

Apothecary My poverty but not my will consents.   75

Romeo   I pay thy poverty and not thy will.

Apothecary Put this in any liquid thing you will[67]

And drink it off,[68] and if you had the strength

Of twenty men, it would dispatch[69] you straight.

Romeo   There is thy gold – worse poison to men's souls,   80

Doing more murder in this loathsome world,

Than these poor compounds that thou mayst not sell.

I sell[70] thee poison; thou hast sold me none.

Farewell. Buy food and get thyself in flesh.

(*to the poison*) Come, cordial[71] and not poison, go with me   85

To Juliet's grave, for there must I use thee.

EXEUNT

65 gives, supplies, grants
66 the law
67 wish to
68 drink it off = drink all of it
69 kill
70 give / hand / deliver to
71 restorative

SCENE 2

Verona. Friar Laurence's cell

ENTER FRIAR JOHN

John Holy Franciscan friar, brother, ho!

ENTER FRIAR LAURENCE

Friar (*entering*) This same should be the voice of Friar John.
(*seeing Friar John*) Welcome from Mantua. What says Romeo?
Or, if his mind[1] be writ, give me his letter.

5 *John* Going[2] to find a barefoot brother out,[3]
One of our order, to associate me,[4]
Here in this city visiting the sick,
And finding him, the searchers of the town,[5]
Suspecting that we both were in a house[6]

10 Where the infectious pestilence[7] did reign,[8]
Sealed up the doors, and would not let us forth,[9]
So that my speed[10] to Mantua there was stayed.[11]

Friar Who bore my letter, then, to Romeo?

John I could not send it – here it is again –

15 Nor get a messenger to bring it thee,

---

1 thought, intention
2 after going
3 find a barefoot brother out = search for a barefoot brother
4 associate me = join with me (friars not being allowed to travel alone)
5 searchers of the town = public officials who located plague sites
6 religious house (monastery or convent)
7 plague
8 did reign = flourished, was prevalent
9 go away, come out
10 swift progress
11 halted

So fearful were they of infection.
Friar Unhappy fortune![12] By my brotherhood,
The letter was not nice,[13] but full of charge,[14]
Of dear import,[15] and the neglecting it[16]
May do much danger.[17] Friar John, go hence,   20
Get me an iron crow[18] and bring it straight
Unto my cell.
John   Brother, I'll go and bring it thee.

EXIT

Friar Now must I to the monument alone.
Within this three hours will fair Juliet wake.
She will beshrew me much that Romeo   25
Hath had no notice of these accidents,[19]
But I will write again to Mantua,
And keep her at my cell till Romeo come –
Poor living corse, closed[20] in a dead man's tomb!

EXIT

12 unhappy fortune! = wretched/miserable/unlucky chance/accident
13 foolish, trivial
14 weight, importance
15 dear import = grievous significance
16 neglecting it = failure to do it
17 harm, damage
18 crowbar
19 occurrences, events (especially of an unfortunate nature)
20 shut, confined

SCENE 3

Verona. A churchyard. The monument of the Capulets

ENTER PARIS AND HIS PAGE WITH FLOWERS AND A TORCH

Paris Give me thy torch, boy. Hence,[1] and stand aloof.[2]
Yet put it[3] out, for I would not[4] be seen.
Under yond yew tree[5] lay thee all along,[6]
Holding thine ear close to the hollow[7] ground,
5   So shall no foot upon the churchyard tread,
Being[8] loose, unfirm, with[9] digging up of graves,
But thou shalt hear it. Whistle then to me,
As signal that thou hear'st something approach.
Give me those flowers. Do as I bid thee, go.
10 *Page* (*aside*) I am almost afraid to stand alone
Here in the churchyard, yet I will adventure.

HE RETIRES

Paris Sweet flower,[10] with flowers thy bridal bed I strew –
O woe, thy canopy[11] is dust and stones –
Which with sweet[12] water nightly I will dew,[13]

1 go off / away
2 (1) at some distance, (2) apart from whatever happens
3 the burning torch
4 would not = do not wish
5 yew tree: associated with sadness, perhaps for its very dark green foliage;
   often planted in churchyards
6 all along = lengthwise, at full length
7 excavated (dug up for graves)
8 the churchyard being
9 from, because of
10 Juliet
11 covering over a ceremonial procession
12 fragrant, scented
13 (verb)

Or wanting[14] that, with tears distilled[15] by moans.   15
The obsequies[16] that I for thee will keep
Nightly shall be to strew thy grave and weep.

PAGE WHISTLES

The boy gives warning something doth approach.
What cursèd foot wanders this way tonight
To cross[17] my obsequies and true love's rite?   20
What, with a torch? Muffle[18] me, night, awhile.

RETIRES

ENTER ROMEO AND BALTHASAR WITH A TORCH,
A MATTOCK,[19] AND AN IRON CROWBAR

Romeo Give me that mattock and the wrenching[20] iron.
    Hold, take this letter. Early in the morning
    See thou deliver it to my lord and father.
    Give me the light. Upon thy life I charge thee,   25
    Whate'er thou hearest or seest, stand all aloof
    And do not interrupt me in my course.
    Why I descend into this bed of death
    Is partly to behold my lady's face,
    But chiefly to take thence from her dead finger   30
    A precious ring, a ring that I must use
    In dear employment.[21] Therefore hence, be gone.

14 failing, lacking
15 purified, concentrated
16 funeral rites / ceremonies
17 oppose, thwart
18 conceal, envelop
19 tool for digging in hard ground (similar to a pick-axe)
20 used for twisting: the crowbar
21 dear employment = important / honorable matters / business

But if thou, jealous,[22] dost[23] return to pry[24]

In what I farther[25] shall intend to do,

35 By heaven, I will tear thee joint by joint

And strew this hungry[26] churchyard with thy limbs.

The time and my intents are savage wild,[27]

More fierce and more inexorable[28] far

Than empty[29] tigers or the roaring sea.

40 *Balthasar* I will be gone, sir, and not trouble you.

Romeo So[30] shalt thou show me friendship.[31] (*gives him money*) Take thou that.

Live, and be prosperous, and farewell, good fellow.

Balthasar (*aside*) For all this same,[32] I'll hide me hereabout.

His looks I fear, and his intents I doubt.[33]

RETIRES

45 *Romeo* Thou detestable[34] maw,[35] thou womb[36] of death,

Gorged[37] with the dearest[38] morsel[39] of the earth,

22 mistrustful, doubtful, suspicious
23 do
24 spy, peer, observe more closely
25 in addition
26 hungry: a burial place is "hungry" for corpses
27 savage wild = horribly fierce
28 relentless (inEXorABle)
29 unfed, hungry
30 thus
31 a friendly act/favor/assistance
32 for all this same = despite what he says/has given me
33 mistrust, suspect
34 (DEEtesTAble)
35 throat, stomach
36 belly-like cavity
37 stuffed, glutted
38 most glorious/beloved/precious
39 a choice dish/snack/small meal

Thus I enforce[40] thy rotten jaws to open,

And in despite[41] I'll cram[42] thee with more food.[43]

ROMEO OPENS THE TOMB

Paris   This is that banished haughty Montague

That murdered my love's cousin – with which grief   50

It is supposèd the fair creature died –

And here is come to do some villainous shame[44]

To the dead bodies. I will apprehend[45] him.

(*to Romeo*) Stop thy unhallowed toil,[46] vile Montague.

Can vengeance be pursu'd further than death?   55

Condemnèd villain, I do apprehend thee.

Obey, and go with me, for thou must die.

Romeo I must indeed, and therefore came I hither.

Good gentle youth, tempt not a desperate man.

Fly hence and leave me. Think upon these gone,[47]   60

Let them affright thee. I beseech thee, youth,

Put not another sin upon my head

By urging[48] me to fury. O be gone.

By heaven, I love thee better than myself,

For I come hither armed against myself.   65

Stay not, be gone. Live, and hereafter say

---

40 force, compel
41 contempt, scorn, defiance
42 stuff (verb)
43 more food = an additional meal (himself)
44 villainous shame = wicked/depraved/vile indecency, disgraceful/offensive
   deed
45 seize, arrest
46 unhallowed toil = profane/wicked/impious labor
47 these gone = the corpses in the tomb (now displayed)
48 pressing, pushing, spurring

A madman's mercy bid thee run away.

Paris I do defy thy conjuration[49]

And apprehend thee for a felon[50] here.

70 *Romeo* Wilt thou provoke me? Then have at thee, boy!

THEY FIGHT

Page O Lord, they fight! I will go call the watch.

EXIT PAGE

PARIS FALLS

Paris O I am slain! If thou be merciful,

Open the tomb, lay me with Juliet.

HE DIES

Romeo In faith, I will. Let me peruse[51] this face.

75 Mercutio's kinsman, noble County Paris!

What said my man[52] when my betossèd[53] soul

Did not attend him as we rode? I think

He told me Paris should have[54] married Juliet.

Said he not so? Or did I dream it so?

80 Or am I mad, hearing him talk of Juliet

To think it was so? (*to Paris*) O give me thy hand,

One writ with[55] me in sour misfortune's book.

49 (1) appeal, solemn charge, (2) trick (CONjurAtiON)
50 (1) wretch, villain, (2) convicted criminal
51 inspect, examine
52 what said my man = what did my servant say
53 agitated, disturbed
54 should have = was supposed to have
55 writ with = recorded/inscribed ("written") along with

I'll bury thee in a triumphant[56] grave.
A grave? O no, a lantern,[57] slaughtered youth,
For here lies Juliet, and her beauty makes   85
This vault a feasting presence[58] full of light.
Death, lie thou there, by a dead man interred.[59]

LAYS PARIS IN THE TOMB

(*to and of himself*) How oft when men are at the point of
death
Have they been merry! Which their keepers[60] call
A light'ning[61] before[62] death. O how may I   90
Call this a light'ning? (*to Juliet*) O my love, my wife,
Death that hath sucked the honey of thy breath
Hath had no power yet upon thy beauty.
Thou art not conquered. Beauty's ensign[63] yet
Is crimson in thy lips and in thy cheeks,   95
And death's pale flag is not advancèd[64] there.
Tybalt, liest thou there in thy bloody sheet?[65]
O what more favor can I do to thee
Than with that hand[66] that cut thy youth in twain[67]

56 victor's, conqueror's
57 (1) transparent case, enclosing and illuminated by a light, (2) top of a
   lighthouse, (3) structure with glazed light-admitting apertures/windows
58 feasting presence = banqueting/celebratory place
59 deposited, buried
60 custodians, guards
61 revival ("lightening")
62 BEEfore
63 sign, flag, emblem
64 raised, lifted
65 burial shroud ("winding sheet")
66 his own hand
67 two

100 To sunder[68] his that was thine enemy?
Forgive me, cousin.[69] Ah, dear Juliet,
Why art thou yet so fair? Shall I believe
That unsubstantial[70] Death is amorous,
And that the lean abhorrèd monster keeps
105 Thee here in dark to be his paramour?[71]
For fear of that I still will stay with thee
And never from this palace[72] of dim night
Depart again. Here, here will I remain
With worms[73] that are thy chambermaids. O here
110 Will I set up my everlasting rest
And shake[74] the yoke of inauspicious stars[75]
From this world-wearied flesh.[76] (*to himself*) Eyes, look your
last.
Arms, take your last embrace! (*embracing Juliet*) And lips,
O you
The doors of breath, seal with a righteous kiss
115 A dateless bargain to engrossing Death.[77] (*kisses Juliet*)
(*to the poison*) Come, bitter conduct,[78] come, unsavory[79]
guide,

68 put an end to, cut off
69 Tybalt (cousin by marriage)
70 without body / material substance
71 lady love, mistress
72 (1) storehouse, (2) palatial / stately mansion
73 with worms = together with the worms / maggots
74 flee, be free of
75 yoke of inauspicious stars = fetters / chains of ill omened / malign
astrological influences
76 this world-wearied flesh = this flesh (himself) tired of the living world
77 dateless bargain to engrossing Death = eternal sale (of himself) to all-
purchasing / greedy
78 bitter conduct = painful / grievous / afflicting escort
79 disagreeable, unpleasant, distasteful, offensive

Thou desperate pilot, now at once run on
The dashing[80] rocks thy seasick weary bark.[81]
Here's to my love! (*drinks*) O true apothecary!
Thy drugs are quick. Thus with a kiss I die. 120

HE FALLS

ENTER FRIAR LAURENCE, WITH LANTERN,
CROWBAR, AND SPADE

Friar   Saint Francis be my speed.[82] How oft tonight
Have my old feet stumbled at[83] graves. Who's there?

Balthasar Here's one, a friend, and one that knows you well.

Friar   Bliss[84] be upon you. Tell me, good my friend,
What torch is yond[85] that vainly[86] lends his light 125
To grubs[87] and eyeless skulls? As I discern,[88]
It burneth in the Capels' monument.

Balthasar It doth so, holy sir, and there's my master,[89]
One that you love.

Friar   Who is it?

Balthasar   Romeo.

Friar   How long hath he been there?

Balthasar   Full half an hour. 130

Friar   Go with me to the vault.

Balthasar   I dare not, sir.

80 violently splashed
81 (himself: like a ship, he is bearing/carrying the poison)
82 help, assistance (see *1 Henry IV* 3.1.189, "Good manners be your speed!")
83 on
84 felicity, joy
85 that one over there ("yonder")
86 pointlessly, uselessly
87 maggots
88 as I discern = as well as I can see/tell
89 there's my master = in there is my master

My master knows not but[90] I am gone hence,
And fearfully[91] did menace me with death
If I did stay to look on his intents.[92]

135 *Friar*   Stay, then, I'll go alone. Fear comes upon me.
O much I fear some ill unthrifty[93] thing.

Balthasar As I did sleep under this yew tree here,
I dreamt my master and another fought,
And that my master slew him.

Friar   Romeo![94]

140 Alack, alack, what[95] blood is this which stains
The stony[96] entrance of this sepulcher?
What mean[97] these masterless[98] and gory swords
To lie discolored by this place of peace?[99]

ENTERS THE TOMB

Romeo! O pale! Who else? What, Paris too?
145 And steeped[100] in blood? Ah, what an unkind[101] hour
Is guilty of this lamentable chance?[102]
The lady stirs.

JULIET RISES

90 knows not but = thinks/believes that
91 dreadfully, terribly
92 plans, projects, purposes
93 harmful, wasteful
94 exclamation of surprise/shock (hearing what Romeo has done)
95 whose
96 stone
97 what mean = what does it mean that
98 without a master/owner
99 eternal peace, not worldly
100 soaked
101 unnatural
102 accident, mishap

Juliet O comfortable[103] friar, where is my lord?
    I do remember well where I should[104] be,
    And there I am. Where is my Romeo?   150
Friar I hear some noise. Lady, come from that nest
    Of death, contagion,[105] and unnatural sleep.
    A greater power than we can contradict
    Hath thwarted our intents. Come, come away.
    Thy husband in thy bosom[106] there lies dead,   155
    And Paris too. Come, I'll dispose of[107] thee
    Among a sisterhood of holy nuns.
    Stay not to question, for the watch is coming.
    Come, go, good Juliet. I dare no longer stay.
Juliet Go, get thee hence, for I will not away.   160

EXIT FRIAR

    What's here? A cup, closed in my true love's hand?
    Poison, I see, hath been his timeless[108] end.
    O churl.[109] Drunk all, and left no friendly drop
    To help me after?[110] I will kiss thy lips.
    Haply[111] some poison yet doth hang on them   165
    To make me die with a restorative.[112]

103 reassuring, cheering (COMforTAble)
104 am supposed to
105 sickness, plague
106 in thy bosom = lying against your body
107 dispose of = place (verb)
108 premature, badly timed
109 (1) rude/uncouth person, (2) miser
110 come after you
111 perhaps
112 with a restorative = from/by means of a repayment/restitution (for his not
    having left any poison for her)

KISSES HIM

Thy lips are warm!

Watchman 1 (*within*)   Lead, boy. Which way?

Juliet   Yea, noise? Then I'll be brief. O happy[113] dagger.

SNATCHES ROMEO'S DAGGER

This[114] is thy sheath. There rest, and let me die.

SHE STABS HERSELF AND FALLS ON ROMEO'S BODY

ENTER PAGE AND WATCHMAN

170 *Page*   This is the place. There, where the torch doth burn.

Watchman 1 The ground is bloody. Search about the churchyard.
Go, some of you. Whoe'er you find attach.[115]

EXEUNT SOME OF THE WATCH

Pitiful sight! Here lies the County slain,
And Juliet bleeding, warm, and newly dead,
175   Who here hath lain this two days burièd.
Go tell the Prince, run to the Capulets,
Raise up the Montagues. Some others search.

EXEUNT OTHERS OF THE WATCH

We see the ground[116] whereon these woes[117] do lie,
But the true ground[118] of all these piteous woes

113 lucky, opportune, appropriate
114 her body
115 arrest, seize
116 earth
117 (1) miseries, misfortunes, (2) miserable/unfortunate bodies/corpses
118 foundation, basis, explanation

We cannot without circumstance[119] descry.[120]   180

ENTER SOME OF THE WATCH, WITH BALTHASAR

Watchman 2 Here's Romeo's man. We found him in the
churchyard.
Watchman 1 Hold him in safety[121] till the Prince come hither.

ENTER FRIAR LAURENCE AND ANOTHER WATCHMAN

Watchman 3 Here is a friar that trembles, sighs, and weeps.
We took this mattock and this spade from him
As he was coming from this churchyard side.[122]   185
Watchman 1 A great suspicion.[123] Stay the friar too.

ENTER THE PRINCE, WITH ATTENDANTS

Prince   What misadventure[124] is so early up,[125]
That calls our person[126] from our morning rest?

ENTER CAPULET AND LADY CAPULET, WITH OTHERS

Capulet   What should[127] it be, that they so shriek
abroad?[128]
Lady Capulet The people in the street cry "Romeo,"   190
Some "Juliet," and some "Paris," and all run,

119 context, causes, reasons
120 discover, detect, perceive
121 close / secure custody
122 this churchyard side = this side of the churchyard
123 great suspicion = large / weighty ground for suspicion
124 bad fortune
125 (1) out of bed, risen, (2) started, stirring, in progress
126 our person = me
127 might, must
128 shriek abroad = cry out / scream everywhere / all over

With open outcry,[129] toward our monument.

Prince   What fear is this which startles[130] in our ears?

Watchman 1   Sovereign, here lies the County Paris slain,

195   And Romeo dead, and Juliet, dead before,

Warm and new killed.

Prince   Search, seek, and know how this foul murder comes.

Watchman 1   Here is a friar, and slaughtered Romeo's man,[131]

With instruments[132] upon them fit to open[133]

200   These dead men's tombs.

Capulet   O heavens! O wife, look how our daughter bleeds![134]

This dagger hath mista'en,[135] for, lo, his house[136]

Is empty on the back[137] of Montague,[138]

And it missheathèd in my daughter's bosom.

205 *Lady Capulet*   O me! this sight of death is as a bell

That warns[139] my old age to[140] a sepulcher.

ENTER MONTAGUE, WITH OTHERS

Prince   Come, Montague, for thou art early up

---

129 open outcry = general/universal/uncontrolled hue and cry
130 starts up, shocks, stuns
131 slaughtered Romeo's man = servant of dead Romeo
132 tools
133 fit to open = suitable for opening
134 (as bodies dead for some while do not bleed)
135 made an error/mistake
136 his house = the dagger's housing/sheath
137 on the back: swords were worn on the side, daggers at the belt, in back
138 Romeo
139 (1) informs, makes known to, (2) describes, (3) instructs, teaches
140 of, about

To see thy son and heir more early down.[141]

Montague Alas, my liege,[142] my wife is dead tonight.[143]

Grief of[144] my son's exile hath stopped her breath.   210

What further woe conspires against mine age?[145]

Prince   Look, and thou shalt see.

Montague (to Romeo) O thou untaught![146] What[147] manners is in this,

To press[148] before thy father to a grave?

Prince   Seal up the mouth[149] of outrage[150] for a while,   215

Till we can clear these ambiguities[151]

And know their spring,[152] their head,[153] their true descent,[154]

And then will I be general[155] of your woes

And lead you, even to death.[156] Meantime forbear,

And let mischance be slave to patience.[157]   220

---

141 fallen
142 lord
143 is dead tonight = died last night
144 grief of = the grief of, grief for
145 old age
146 ignorant, unenlightened
147 what sort/kind of
148 thrust, push
149 the mouth = tomb opening
150 violent/passionate lamentation
151 doubts, uncertainties
152 source (as of a stream)
153 origin (conception, as of an idea)
154 derivation, line of descent (as of a lineage proceeding from generation to generation)
155 person in charge
156 the death of whoever is responsible
157 mischance be slave to patience = disaster/calamity be subject to/ dominated by patience

Bring forth the parties of suspicion.[158]

Friar   I am the greatest,[159] able to do least,
Yet most suspected, as the time and place
Doth make[160] against me, of this direful murder,
225   And here I stand, both to impeach and purge[161]
Myself condemnèd[162] and myself excused.[163]

Prince   Then say it once[164] what thou dost know in this.

Friar   I will be brief, for my short date of breath[165]
Is not so long as is a tedious tale.
230   Romeo, there dead, was husband to that Juliet,
And she, there dead, that Romeo's faithful wife.
I married them, and their stol'n[166] marriage day
Was Tybalt's doomsday,[167] whose untimely death
Banished the new made bridegroom from this city,
235   For whom – and not for Tybalt – Juliet pined.[168]
(*to Capulet*) You, to remove that siege[169] of grief from her,
Betrothed and would have married her perforce
To County Paris. Then comes she to me
And with wild looks bid me devise some mean[170]

---

158 parties of suspicion = suspected persons
159 principal one
160 produce/cause suspicion
161 impeach and purge = accuse and clear
162 called guilty
163 freed from blame
164 once and for all, in short
165 date of breath = time/length of life
166 secret
167 death day
168 grieved, suffered, longed for
169 period of illness/difficulty
170 way ("means")

To rid[171] her from this second marriage,   240
Or in my cell there[172] would she kill herself.
Then gave I her, so tutored[173] by my art,
A sleeping potion, which so[174] took effect
As I intended, for it wrought[175] on her
The form[176] of death. Meantime I writ to Romeo   245
That he should hither come as[177] this dire night
To help to take her from her borrowed grave,
Being the time the potion's force should cease.
But he which[178] bore my letter, Friar John,
Was stayed by accident, and yesternight   250
Returned[179] my letter back. Then all alone
At the prefixèd[180] hour of her waking
Came I to take her from her kindred's vault,
Meaning to keep her closely[181] at my cell
Till I conveniently[182] could send[183] to Romeo.   255
But when I came, some minute ere the time
Of her awaking, here untimely lay
The noble Paris and true Romeo dead.

171 free
172 in that case, then ("then and there")
173 taught, instructed
174 accordingly, thus, then
175 worked
176 visible appearance/likeness
177 precisely/exactly on ("at the time of")
178 who
179 brought
180 appointed, previously set
181 privately, secretly
182 properly, appropriately
183 send a message/messenger

She wakes,[184] and I entreated[185] her come[186] forth

260   And bear this work[187] of heaven with patience.

But then a noise did scare me from the tomb,

And she, too desperate, would not go with me,

But, as it seems, did violence on herself.

All this I know,[188] and to the marriage

265   Her nurse is privy.[189] And if aught in this

Miscarried[190] by my fault, let my old life

Be sacrificed, some hour before his[191] time,

Unto[192] the rigor[193] of severest law.

Prince   We still have known thee for a holy man.

270   Where's Romeo's man? What can he say in this?

Balthasar   I brought my master news of Juliet's death,

And then in post he came from Mantua

To this same place, to this same monument.

This letter he early[194] bid me give his father,

275   And threatened me with death, going[195] in the vault,

If I departed not[196] and left him there.

Prince   Give me the letter. I will look on[197] it.

---

184 woke
185 asked, begged
186 to come
187 act, deed
188 (he has knowledge, as opposed to mere belief)
189 (1) cognizant, aware, (2) intimately acquainted / involved
190 came to harm, went wrong
191 its
192 according to, to the limit of
193 strictness, harshness
194 at the beginning / the start
195 should I go
196 departed not = did not leave
197 at

Where is the County's page that raised[198] the watch?
(*to Page*) Sirrah, what made your master[199] in this place?

Page   He came with flowers to strew his lady's grave,   280
And bid me stand aloof, and so I did.
Anon comes one with light to ope[200] the tomb,
And by and by my master drew[201] on him,
And then I ran away to call the watch.

Prince   This letter doth make good the friar's words,   285
Their course of love, the tidings[202] of her death,
And here he writes that he did buy a poison
Of[203] a poor pothecary,[204] and therewithal[205]
Came to this vault to die, and lie with Juliet.
Where be these enemies? Capulet, Montague,   290
See what a scourge[206] is laid upon[207] your hate,
That heaven finds means to kill your joys with love.
And I, for winking at your discords too,
Have lost a brace[208] of kinsmen. All are punished.

Capulet O brother Montague, give me thy hand.   295
This is my daughter's jointure,[209] for no more
Can I demand.[210]

---

198 roused, called
199 what made your master = what was your master doing
200 open
201 drew his sword
202 news
203 from
204 apothecary
205 (1) with that, (2) in addition
206 whip, lash, punishment
207 laid upon = brought down/put on, applied to
208 pair
209 sum left to wife if husband predeceases her
210 claim

Montague But I can give thee more,
　　　For I will raise[211] her statue[212] in pure gold,
300　　　That whiles[213] Verona by that name is known
　　　There shall no figure[214] at such rate[215] be set
　　　As that of true and faithful Juliet.
Capulet　As rich shall Romeo's[216] by his lady's lie,[217]
　　　Poor sacrifices of our enmity.[218]
305 *Prince*　A glooming[219] peace this morning with it brings.
　　　The sun for sorrow will not show his head.
　　　Go hence, to have more talk of these sad things.
　　　Some shall be pardoned, and some punishèd,
　　　For never was a story of more woe
310　　　Than this of Juliet and her Romeo.

EXEUNT OMNES

211 set up, build, construct
212 image, effigy
213 during the time, as long as
214 (1) person's appearance, (2) image/representation ("statue") of a person's
　　appearance
215 value
216 Romeo's statue
217 be located/situated, remain (in modern usage, statues *stand:* these however
　　are "images, effigies" and planned to be horizontal, not vertical)
218 (ENmiTY – the final syllable pronounced like modern "tie")
219 sullen, melancholy, dark

Shakespeare's first authentic tragedy has sometimes been critically undervalued, perhaps because of its popularity. Though *Romeo and Juliet* is a triumph of dramatic lyricism, its tragic ending usurps most other aspects of the play and abandons us to unhappy estimates of whether, and to what degree, its young lovers are responsible for their own catastrophe. Harold Goddard lamented that the Prologue's "A pair of star-cross'd lovers take their life" had "surrendered this drama to the astrologers," though more than the stars in their courses are to blame for the destruction of the superb Juliet. Alas, half a century after Goddard, the tragedy more frequently is surrendered to commissars of gender and power, who can thrash the patriarchy, including Shakespeare himself, for victimizing Juliet.

Thomas McAlindon in his refreshingly sane *Shakespeare's Tragic Cosmos* (1991) traces the dynamics of conflict in the dramatist back to the rival worldviews of Heraclitus and Empedocles, as refined and modified in Geoffrey Chaucer's *The Knight's Tale*. For Heraclitus, all things flowed, as Empedocles visualized a strife between Love and Death. Chaucer, rather than Ovid or Christopher Marlowe, was the ancestor of Shakespeare's greatest originality, that invention of the human. Chaucer's ironic yet amiable version of the religion of love, more perhaps in his *Troilus and Criseyde* than in *The Knight's Tale,* is the essential context for *Romeo and Juliet.* Time's ironies govern love in Chaucer, as they will in *Romeo and Juliet.* Chaucer's human nature is essentially Shakespeare's: the deepest link between the two greatest English poets was temperamental rather than intellectual or sociopolitical. Love dies or else lovers die: those are the pragmatic possibilities for the two poets, each of them experientially wise beyond wisdom.

Shakespeare, somewhat unlike Chaucer, shied away from depicting the death of love rather than the death of lovers. Does anyone, except Hamlet, ever fall out of love in Shakespeare? Hamlet denies anyway that he ever loved Ophelia, and I believe him. By the time the play ends, he loves no one, whether it be the dead Ophelia or the dead father, the dead Gertrude or the dead Yorick, and one wonders if this frightening charismatic ever could have loved anyone. If there were an act 6 to Shakespeare's comedies, doubtless many of the concluding marriages would approximate the condition of Shakespeare's own union with Anne Hathaway. My observation, of course, is nonsensical if you would have it so, but most of the Shakespearean audience—then, now, and always—goes on believing that Shakespeare uniquely represented realities. Poor Falstaff never will stop loving Hal, and the admirably Christian Antonio always will pine for Bassanio. Whom Shakespeare himself loved we do not know, but the Sonnets seem more than a fiction and, at least in this aspect of life, Shakespeare evidently was not so cold as his Hamlet.

There are mature lovers in Shakespeare, most notably Antony and Cleopatra, who cheerfully sell each other out for reasons of state, yet return to each other in their suicides. Both Romeo and

Antony kill themselves because they falsely think their beloveds are dead (Antony bungles the suicide, as he does everything else). The most passionate marriage in Shakespeare, the Macbeths', subtly appears to have its sexual difficulties and ends in madness and suicide for Queen Macbeth, prompting the most equivocal of elegiac reflections by her usurping husband. "Yet Edmund was belov'd," the icy villain of *King Lear* overhears himself saying, when the bodies of Goneril and Regan are brought in.

The varieties of passionate love between the sexes are endlessly Shakespeare's concern; sexual jealousy finds its most flamboyant artists in Othello and Leontes, but the virtual identity of the torments of love and jealousy is a Shakespearean invention, later to be refined by Nathaniel Hawthorne and Marcel Proust. Shakespeare, more than any other author, has instructed the West in the catastrophes of sexuality, and has invented the formula that the sexual becomes the erotic when crossed by the shadow of death. There had to be one high song of the erotic by Shakespeare, one lyrical and tragicomical paean celebrating an unmixed love and lamenting its inevitable destruction. *Romeo and Juliet* is unmatched, in Shakespeare and in the world's literature, as a vision of an uncompromising mutual love that perishes of its own idealism and intensity.

There are a few isolated instances of realistic distincts in Shakespeare's characters before *Romeo and Juliet:* Launce in *The Two Gentlemen of Verona,* the Bastard Faulconbridge in *King John,* Richard II, self-destructive king and superb metaphysical poet. The fourfold of Juliet, Mercutio, the Nurse, and Romeo outnumber and overgo these earlier breakthroughs in human invention. *Romeo and Juliet* matters, as a play, because of these four exuberantly realized characters.

It is easier to see the vividness of Mercutio and the Nurse than it is to absorb and sustain the erotic greatness of Juliet and the heroic effort of Romeo to approximate her sublime state of being in love. Shakespeare, with a prophetic insight, knows that he must lead his audience beyond Mercutio's obscene ironies if they are to be worthy of apprehending Juliet, for her sublimity *is* the play and guarantees the tragedy of this tragedy. Mercutio, the scene stealer of the play, had to be killed off if it was to remain Juliet's and Romeo's play; keep Mercutio in acts 4 and 5, and the contention of love and death would have to cease. We overinvest in Mercutio because he insures us against our own erotic eagerness for doom; he is in the play to some considerable purpose. So, in an even darker way, is the Nurse, who helps guarantee the final disaster. The Nurse and Mercutio, both of them audience favorites, are nevertheless bad news, in different but complementary ways. Shakespeare, at this point in his career, may have underestimated his burgeoning powers, because Mercutio and the Nurse go on seducing audiences, readers, directors, and critics. Their verbal exuberances make them forerunners of Touchstone and Jacques, rancid ironists, but also of the dangerously eloquent manipulative villains Iago and Edmund.

Shakespeare's greatness began with *Love's Labour's Lost* (1594–95, revised 1597) and *Richard II* (1595), superb achievements respectively in comedy and in history. Yet *Romeo and Juliet* (1595–96) has rightly overshadowed both, though I cannot quite place it for eminence with *A Midsummer Night's Dream,* composed simultaneously with Shakespeare's first serious tragedy. The permanent popularity, now of mythic intensity, of *Romeo and Juliet* is more than justified, since the play is the largest and most persuasive celebration of romantic love in Western literature. When I think of the play, without rereading and teaching it, or attending yet one more inadequate performance, I first remember neither the tragic outcome nor the gloriously vivid Mercutio and the Nurse. My mind goes directly to the vital center, act 2, scene 2, with its incandescent exchange between the lovers:

> *Romeo* Lady, by yonder blessèd moon I swear,
>   That tips with silver all these fruit-tree tops –
> *Juliet*   O swear not by the moon, th' inconstant moon,
>   That monthly changes in her circled orb,
>   Lest that thy love prove likewise variable.
> *Romeo* What shall I swear by?
> *Juliet*   Do not swear at all,
>   Or if thou wilt, swear by thy gracious self,
>   Which is the god of my idolatry,
>   And I'll believe thee.
> *Romeo*   If my heart's dear love –
> *Juliet*   Well, do not swear. Although I joy in thee,
>   I have no joy of this contract tonight.
>   It is too rash, too unadvised, too sudden,
>   Too like the lightening, which doth cease to be
>   Ere one can say "It lightens." Sweet, good night.
>   This bud of love, by summer's ripening breath,
>   May prove a beauteous flower when next we meet.
>   Good night, good night. As sweet repose and rest
>   Come to thy heart as that within my breast.
> *Romeo* O wilt thou leave me so unsatisfied?
> *Juliet*   What satisfaction canst thou have tonight?
> *Romeo* Th' exchange of thy love's faithful vow for mine.

Juliet   I gave thee mine before thou didst request it,
    And yet I would it were to give again.
Romeo Wouldst thou withdraw it? For what purpose, love?
Juliet   But to be frank and give it thee again.
    And yet I wish but for the thing I have.
    My bounty is as boundless as the sea,
    My love as deep. The more I give to thee,
    The more I have, for both are infinite.

[2.2.107–35]

The revelation of Juliet's nature here might be called an epiphany in the religion of love. Chaucer has nothing like this, nor does Dante, since his Beatrice's love for him transcends sexuality. Unprecedented in literature (though presumably not in life), Juliet precisely does not transcend the human heroine. Whether Shakespeare reinvents the representation of a very young woman (she is not yet fourteen) in love, or perhaps does even more than that, is difficult to decide. How do you distance Juliet? You only shame yourself by bringing irony to a contemplation of her consciousness. William Hazlitt, spurred by a nostalgia for his own lost dreams of love, caught better than any other critic the exact temper of this scene: "He has founded the passion of the two lovers not in the pleasures they had experienced, but on all the pleasures they had *not* experienced."

It is the sense of an infinity yet to come that is evoked by Juliet, nor can we doubt that her bounty is "as boundless as the sea." When Rosalind in *As You Like It* repeats this simile, it is in a tonality that subtly isolates Juliet's difference:

Rosalind O coz, coz, coz, my pretty little coz, that thou didst
    know how many fathoms deep I am in love! But it cannot

be sounded. My affection hath an unknown bottom, like
the Bay of Portugal.

Celia   Or rather bottomless, that as fast as you pour
affection in, it runs out.

Rosalind No. That same wicked bastard of Venus, that was
begot of thought, conceived of spleen and born of
madness, that blind rascally boy that abuses everyone's eyes
because his own are out, let him be judge how deep I am
in love.

[4.1.195–205]

This is the sublimest of female wits, who one imagines would
advise Romeo and Juliet to "die by attorney," and who knows
that women, as well as men, "have died from time to time and
worms have eaten them, but not for love." Romeo and Juliet, alas,
are exceptions, and die for love rather than live for wit. Shakespeare allows nothing like Rosalind's supreme intelligence to in-
trude upon Juliet's authentic rapture. Mercutio, endlessly obscene, is not qualified to darken Juliet's intimations of ecstasy.
The play has already made clear how brief this happiness must be.
Against that context, against also all of his own ironic reserva-
tions, Shakespeare allows Juliet the most exalted declaration of
romantic love in the language:

Juliet But to be frank and give it thee again;
        And yet I wish but for the thing I have.
        My bounty is as boundless as the sea,
        My love as deep: The more I give to thee
        The more I have, for both are infinite.

[2.2.131–35]

We have to measure the rest of this play against these five lines, miraculous in their legitimate pride and poignance. They defy Dr. Johnson's wry remark on Shakespeare's rhetorical extravagances throughout the play: "his pathetick strains are always polluted with some unexpected depravations." Molly Mahood, noting that there are at least 175 puns and allied wordplays in *Romeo and Juliet,* finds them appropriate to a riddling drama where "Death has long been Romeo's rival and enjoys Juliet at the last," an appropriate finale for doom-eager lovers. Yet little in the drama suggests that Romeo and Juliet are in love with death, as well as with each other. Shakespeare stands back from assigning blame, whether to the feuding older generation, or to the lovers, or to fate, time, chance, and the cosmological contraries. Julia Kristeva, rather too courageously not standing back, rushes in to discover "a discreet version of the Japanese *Realm of the Senses,*" a baroque sadomasochistic motion picture.

Clearly Shakespeare took some risks in letting us judge this tragedy for ourselves, but that refusal to usurp his audience's freedom allowed ultimately for the composition of the final high tragedies. I think that I speak for more than myself when I assert that the love shared by Romeo and Juliet is as healthy and normative a passion as Western literature affords us. It concludes in mutual suicide, but not because either of the lovers lusts for death, or mingles hatred with desire.

Mercutio is the most notorious scene stealer in all of Shakespeare, and there is a tradition (reported by John Dryden) that Shakespeare declared he was obliged to kill off Mercutio, lest Mercutio kill Shakespeare and hence the play. Dr. Johnson rightly commended Mercutio for wit, gaiety, and courage; presumably the great critic chose to ignore that Mercutio also is obscene, heart-less, and quarrelsome. Mercutio promises a grand comic role, and yet disturbs us also with his extraordinary rhapsody concerning Queen Mab, who at first seems to belong more to *A Midsummer Night's Dream* than to *Romeo and Juliet:*

> *Mercutio* O then I see Queen Mab hath been with you.
> She is the fairies' midwife, and she comes
> In shape no bigger than an agate stone
> On the forefinger of an alderman,
> Drawn with a team of little atomies
> Athwart men's noses as they lie asleep –
> Her wagon spokes made of long spinners' legs;
> The cover, of the wings of grasshoppers;
> Her traces, of the smallest spider's web,
> Her collars, of the moonshine's wat'ry beams;
> Her whip, of cricket's bone; the lash, of film;
> Her wagoner, a small gray-coated gnat,
> Not half so big as a round little worm
> Pricked from the lazy finger of a maid;
> Her chariot is an empty hazelnut,
> Made by the joiner squirrel or old grub,
> Time out o' mine the fairies' coachmakers.
> And in this state she gallops night by night
> Through lovers' brains, and then they dream of love;
> O'er courtiers' knees, that dream on curtsies straight;
> O'er lawyers' fingers who straight dream on fees;
> O'er ladies' lips, who straight on kisses dream,
> Which oft the angry Mab with blisters plagues
> Because their breaths with sweetmeats tainted are.

Sometimes she gallops o'er a courtier's nose,
And then dreams he of smelling out a suit;
And sometime comes she with a tithe pig's tail
Tickling a parson's nose as 'a lies asleep,
Then dreams he of another benefice.
Sometimes she driveth o'er a soldier's neck
And then dreams he of cutting foreign throats,
Of breaches, ambuscadoes, Spanish blades,
Of healths five fathom deep; and then anon
Drums in his ear, at which he starts and wakes,
And being thus frighted swears a prayer or two
And sleeps again. This is that very Mab
That plats the manes of horses in the night
And bakes the elflocks in foul sluttish hair,
Which once untangled much misfortune bodes.
This is the hag, when maids lie on their backs,
That presses them and learns them first to bear,
Making them women of good carriage.
This is she —

[1.4.53–95]

Romeo interrupts, since clearly Mercutio never stops once started. This mercurial vision of Queen Mab—where "Queen" probably means a whore, and Mab refers to a Celtic fairy, who frequently manifests as a will-o'-the-wisp—is anything but out of character. Mercutio's Mab is the midwife of our erotic dreams, aiding us to give birth to our deep fantasies, and she appears to posses a childlike charm for much of the length of Mercutio's description. But since he is a major instance of what D. H. Lawrence was to call "sex-in-the-head," Mercutio is setting us up for the revelation of Mab as the nightmare, the incubus who impregnates maids. Romeo interrupts to say: "Thou talkst of nothing," where "nothing" is another slang term for the vagina. Mercutio's bawdy obsessiveness is splendidly employed by Shakespeare as a reduction of Romeo and Juliet's honest exaltation of their passion. Directly before their first rendezvous, we hear Mercutio at his most obscenely exuberant pitch:

> If love be blind, love cannot hit the mark.
> Now will he sit under a medlar tree
> And wish his mistress were that kind of fruit
> As maids call medlars when they laugh alone.
> O Romeo, that she were, O that she were
> An open arse, and thou a pop'rin pear!
>
> [2.1.33–38]

Mercutio's reference is to Rosaline, Romeo's beloved before he falls, at first glance, in love with Juliet, who instantly reciprocates. The medlar, rotten with ripeness, popularly was believed to have the likeness of the female genitalia, and "to meddle" meant to perform sexual intercourse. Mercutio happily also cites a popular name for the medlar, the open arse, as well as the pop'rin pear, at once pop-her-in her open arse, and the slang name for a French pear, the Poperingle (named for a town near Ypres). This is the antithetical prelude to a scene that famously concludes with Juliet's couplet:

> Good night, good night. Parting is such sweet sorrow
> That I shall say good night till it be morrow.
>
> [2.2.185–186]

Mercutio at his best is a high-spiritual unbeliever in the religion of love, reductive as he may be:

Benvolio Here comes Romeo, here comes Romeo!

Mercutio Without his roe, like a dried herring. O flesh, flesh, how art thou fishified! Now is he for the numbers that Petrarch flowed in. Laura, to his lady, was but a kitchen wench – marry, she had a better love to berhyme her – Dido a dowdy, Cleopatra a gypsy, Helen and Hero hildings and harlots, Thisbe a gray eye or so, [...]

[2.4.34–40]

Obsessed as he may be, Mercutio has the style to take his death wound as gallantly as anyone in Shakespeare:

Romeo Courage, man, the hurt cannot be much.

Mercutio No, 'tis not so deep as a well, nor so wide as a church door, but 'tis enough, 'twill serve. Ask for me tomorrow and you shall find me a grave man. I am peppered, I warrant, for this world. A plague o' both your houses.

[3.1.91–95]

That indeed is what in his death Mercutio becomes, a plague upon both Romeo of the Montagues and Juliet of the Capulets, since henceforward the tragedy speeds on to its final double catastrophe. Shakespeare is already Shakespeare in his subtle patterning, although rather overlyrical still in his style. The two fatal figures in the play are its two liveliest comics, Mercutio and the Nurse. Mercutio's aggressivity has prepared the destruction of love, though there is no negative impulse in Mercutio, who dies by the tragic irony that Romeo's intervention in the duel with Tybalt is prompted by love for Juliet, a relationship of which Mercutio is totally unaware. Mercutio is victimized by what is most central to the play, and yet he dies without knowing what *Romeo and Juliet* is all about: the tragedy of authentic romantic love. For Mercutio, that is nonsense: love is an open arse and a pop'rin pear. To die as love's martyr, as it were, when you do not believe in the religion of love, and do not even know what you are dying for, is a grotesque irony that foreshadows the dreadful ironies that will destroy Juliet and Romeo alike as the play concludes.

Juliet's Nurse, despite her popularity, is altogether a much darker figure. Like Mercutio, she is inwardly cold, even toward Juliet, whom she has raised. Her language captivates us, as does Mercutio's, but Shakespeare gives both of them hidden natures much at variance with their exuberant personalities. Mercutio's incessant bawdiness is the mask for what may be a repressed homoeroticism, and like his violence may indicate a flight from the acute sensibility at work in the Queen Mab speech until it too transmutes into obscenity. The Nurse is even more complex; her apparent vitalism and her propulsive flood of language beguile us in her first full speech:

> Even or odd, of all days in the year,
> Come Lammas Eve at night shall she be fourteen.
> Susan and she (God rest all Christian souls)
> Were of an age. Well, Susan is with God,
> She was too good for me. But as I said,
> On Lammas Eve at night shall she be fourteen.
> That shall she. Marry, I remember it well.
> 'Tis since the earthquake now eleven years,
> And she was wean'd (I never shall forget it),
> Of all the days of the year, upon that day.
> For I had then laid wormwood to my dug,

Sitting in the sun under the dovehouse wall.
My lord and you were then at Mantua.
Nay, I do bear a brain. But as I said,
When it did taste the wormwood on the nipple
Of my dug and felt it bitter, pretty fool,
To see it tetchy and fall out with the dug!
Shake, quoth the dovehouse! 'Twas no need, I trow,
To bid me trudge.
And since that time it is eleven years.
For then she could stand high lone. Nay, by th' rood,
She could have run and waddled all about;
For even the day before she broke her brow,
And then my husband – God be with his soul,
'A was a merry man – took up the child.
"Yea," quoth he, "dost thou fall upon thy face?
Thou wilt fall backward when thou hast more wit,
Wilt thou not, Jule?" And, by my holidam,
the pretty wretch left crying, and said "Ay."
To see now how a jest shall come about.
I warrant, an I should live a thousand years
I never should forget it. "Wilt thou not, Jule?" quoth he,
And, pretty fool, it stinted and said "Ay."

[1.3.16–48]

Her speech is shrewd and not so simple as first it sounds, and comes short of poignance, because already there is something antipathetic in the Nurse. Juliet, like her late twin sister, Susan, is too good for the Nurse, and there is an edge to the account of the weaning that is bothersome, since we do not hear the accents of love.

Shakespeare delays any more ultimate revelation of the Nurse's nature until the crucial scene where she fails Juliet. The exchanges here need to be quoted at length, because Juliet's shock is a new effect for Shakespeare. The Nurse is the person who has been closest to Juliet for all the fourteen years of her life, and suddenly Juliet realizes that what has seemed loyalty and care is something else.

Juliet   O God, O Nurse, how shall this be prevented?
    My husband is on earth, my faith in heaven.
    How shall that faith return again to earth
    Unless that husband send it me from heaven
    By leaving earth? Comfort me, counsel me.
    Alack, alack, that heaven should practice stratagems
    Upon so soft a subject as myself.
    What say'st thou? Hast thou not a word of joy?
    Some comfort, Nurse.
Nurse   Faith, here it is.
    Romeo is banished, and all the world to nothing
    That he dares ne'er come back to challenge you,
    Or if he do, it needs must be by stealth.
    Then, since the case so stands as now it doth,
    I think it best you married with the County.
    O he's a lovely gentleman.
    Romeo's a dishclout to him. An eagle, madam,
    Hath not so green, so quick, so fair an eye
    As Paris hath. Beshrew my very heart,
    I think you are happy in this second match,
    For it excels your first, or if it did not,
    Your first is dead – or 'twere as good he were
    As living here and you no use of him.

Juliet Speak'st thou from thy heart?

Nurse And from my soul too, else beshrew them both.

Juliet Amen.

Nurse What?

Juliet Well, thou hast comforted me marvelous much.

    Go in, and tell my lady I am gone,

    Having displeased my father, to Laurence cell,

    To make confession and to be absolved.

Nurse Marry, I will, and this is wisely done.

EXIT

Juliet Ancient damnation! O most wicked fiend,

    Is it more sin to wish me thus forsworn,

    Or to dispraise my lord with that same tongue

    Which she hath praised him with above compare

    So many thousand times? Go, counselor.

    Thou and my bosom henceforth shall be twain.

    I'll to the friar to know his remedy.

    If all else fail, myself have power to die.

[3.5.205–43]

The more-than-poignant: "that heaven should practice strat-egems / Upon so soft a subject as myself" is answered by the Nurse's astonishing "comfort": "it excels your first, or if it did not, / Your first is dead." The Nurse's argument is valid if convenience is everything; since Juliet is in love, we hear instead an over-whelming rejection of the Nurse, proceeding from the eloquent "amen" on to the dry: "Well, thou hast comforted me marvelous much." The Nurse indeed is "Ancient damnation! O most wicked fiend," and we will hardly hear from her again until Juliet "dies" her first death in this play. Like Mercutio, the Nurse moves us at last to distrust every apparent value in the tragedy except the lovers' commitment to each other.

Juliet, and not Romeo, or even Brutus in *Julius Caesar,* dies her second death as a prefiguration of Hamlet's charismatic splendor. Romeo, though he changes enormously under her influence, remains subject to anger and to despair, and is as responsible as Mercutio and Tybalt are for the catastrophe. Having slain Tybalt, Romeo cries out that he has become "Fortune's fool." We would wince if Juliet called herself "Fortune's fool," since she is as nearly flawless as her situation allows, and we recall instead her wry prayer: "Be fickle, Fortune." Perhaps any playgoer or any reader remembers best Romeo and Juliet's aubade after their single night of fulfillment:

> *Juliet*   Wilt thou be gone? It is not yet near day.
> It was the nightingale, and not the lark,
> That pierced the fearful hollow of thine ear.
> Nightly she sings on yond pom'granate tree.
> Believe me, love, it was the nightingale.
> *Romeo*   It was the lark, the herald of the morn,
> No nightingale. Look, love, what envious streaks
> Do lace the severing clouds in yonder east.
> Night's candles are burnt out, and jocund day
> Stands tiptoe on the misty mountain tops.
> I must be gone and live, or stay and die.
> *Juliet*   Yond light is not daylight, I know it, I.
> It is some meteor that the sun exhales
> To be to thee this night a torchbearer

And light thee on thy way to Mantua.

Therefore stay yet, thou need'st not to be gone.

Romeo Let me be ta'en, let me be put to death.

I am content, so thou wilt have it so.

I'll say yon gray is not the morning's eye,

'Tis but the pale reflex of Cynthia's brow.

Nor that is not the lark whose notes do beat

The vaulty heaven so high above our heads.

I have more care to stay than will to go.

Come, death, and welcome. Juliet wills it so.

How is't, my soul? Let's talk. It is not day.

Juliet   It is, it is. Hie hence, be gone, away.

It is the lark that sings so out of tune,

Straining harsh discords and unpleasing sharps.

Some say the lark makes sweet division.

This doth not so, for she divideth us.

Some say the lark and loathèd toad change eyes.

O now I would they had changed voices too,

Since arm from arm that voice doth us affray,

Hunting thee hence with "Hunt's up" to the day.

O now be gone, more light and light it grows.

Romeo More light and light, more dark and dark our woes.

[3.5.1–36]

Exquisite in itself, this is also a subtle epitome of the tragedy of this tragedy, for the entire play could be regarded as a dawn song that, alas, is out of phase. A bemused audience, unless the director is shrewd, is likely to become skeptical that event after event arrives in the untimeliest way possible. Romeo and Juliet's aubade is so disturbing precisely because they are not courtly love sophisticates working through a stylized ritual. The courtly lover confronts the possibility of a real-enough death if he lingers too long, because his partner is an adulterous wife. But Juliet and Romeo know that death after dawn would be Romeo's punishment, not for adultery, but merely for marriage. The subtle outrageousness of Shakespeare's drama is that everything is against the lovers: their families and the state, the indifference of nature, the vagaries of time, and the regressive movement of the cosmological contraries of love and strife. Even had Romeo transcended his anger; even if Mercutio and the Nurse were not quarrelsome busybodies, the odds are too great against the triumph of love. That is the aubade's undersong, made explicit in Romeo's great outcry against the contraries: "More light and light, more dark and dark our woes."

What was Shakespeare trying to do for himself as a playwright by composing *Romeo and Juliet?* Tragedy did not come easily to Shakespeare, yet all this play's lyricism and comic genius cannot hold off the dawn that will become a destructive darkness. With just a few alterations, Shakespeare could have transformed *Romeo and Juliet* into a play as cheerful as *A Midsummer Night's Dream.* The young lovers, escaped to Mantua or Padua, would not have been victims of Verona, or of bad timing, or of cosmological contraries asserting their sway. Yet this travesty would have been intolerable for us, and for Shakespeare: a passion as absolute as Romeo's and Juliet's cannot consort with comedy. Mere sexuality will do for comedy, but the shadow of death makes eroticism the companion of tragedy. Shakespeare, in *Romeo and Juliet,* eschews Chaucerian irony, but he takes from *The Knight's Tale* Chaucer's intimation that we are always keeping appointments we haven't made. Here it is the sublime appointment kept by Paris and

Romeo at Juliet's supposed tomb, which soon enough becomes both her authentic tomb and their own. What is left on stage at the close of this tragedy is an absurd pathos: the wretched Friar Laurence, who fearfully abandoned Juliet; a widowed Montague, who vows to have a statue of Juliet raised in pure gold; the Capulets vowing to end a feud already spent in five deaths – those of Mercutio, Tybalt, Paris, Romeo, and Juliet. The closing curtain of any proper production of the play should descend upon these final ironies, presented as ironies, and not as images of reconciliation. As is *Julius Caesar* after it, *Romeo and Juliet* is a training ground in which Shakespeare teaches himself remorselessness and prepares the way for his five great tragedies, starting with the *Hamlet* of 1600–1601.

FURTHER READING

This is not a bibliography but a selective set of starting places.

Texts

Shakespeare, William. *The First Folio of Shakespeare.* 2d ed. Edited by
   Charlton Hinman. Introduction by Peter W. M. Blayney. New York:
   W. W. Norton, 1996.
———. *The Most Excellent and Lamentable Tragedie of Romeo and Juliet:
   A Critical Edition.* Edited by George Walton Williams. Durham, N.C.:
   Duke University Press, 1964.
———. *Romeo and Juliet: A New Variorum Edition.* Edited by Horace
   Howard Furness. New York: Lippincott, 1871. Reprint, New York:
   Dover Books, 1963.
———. *Romeo and Juliet: Four Editions of First and Second Quartos.*
   Edited by P. A. Daniel. London: New Shakspere Society, 1874.
Wells, Stanley, and Gary Taylor, eds. *William Shakespeare: The Complete
   Works.* Oxford: Clarendon Press, 1993.

Language

Dobson, E. J. *English Pronunciation, 1500–1700.* 2d ed. Oxford: Oxford
   University Press, 1968.
Houston, John Porter. *The Rhetoric of Poetry in the Renaissance and
   Seventeenth Century.* Baton Rouge: Louisiana State University Press,
   1983.

————. *Shakespearean Sentences: A Study in Style and Syntax.* Baton Rouge: Louisiana State University Press, 1988.

Kermode, Frank. *Shakespeare's Language.* New York: Farrar, Straus and Giroux, 2000.

Kökeritz, Helge. *Shakespeare's Pronunciation.* New Haven: Yale University Press, 1953.

Lanham, Richard A. *The Motives of Eloquence: Literary Rhetoric in the Renaissance.* New Haven and London: Yale University Press, 1976.

Onions, C. T. *A Shakespeare Glossary.* Enlarged and revised by Robert D. Eagleson. Oxford: Clarendon Press, 1986.

The Oxford English Dictionary: Second Edition on CD-ROM, version 3.0. New York: Oxford University Press, 2002.

Raffel, Burton. *From Stress to Stress: An Autobiography of English Prosody.* Hamden, Conn.: Archon Books, 1992.

Ronberg, Gert. *A Way with Words: The Language of English Renaissance Literature.* London: Arnold, 1992.

Trousdale, Marion. *Shakespeare and the Rhetoricians.* Chapel Hill: University of North Carolina Press, 1982.

Culture

Bindoff, S. T. *Tudor England.* Baltimore: Penguin, 1950.

Bradbrook, M. C. *Shakespeare: The Poet in His World.* New York: Columbia University Press, 1978.

Brown, Cedric C., ed. *Patronage, Politics, and Literary Tradition in England, 1558–1658.* Detroit, Mich.: Wayne State University Press, 1993.

Bush, Douglas. *Prefaces to Renaissance Literature.* New York: W. W. Norton, 1965.

Buxton, John. *Elizabethan Taste.* London: Harvester, 1963.

Cowan, Alexander. *Urban Europe, 1500–1700.* New York: Oxford University Press, 1998.

Driver, Tom E. *The Sense of History in Greek and Shakespearean Drama.* New York: Columbia University Press, 1960.

Finucci, Valeria, and Regina Schwartz, eds. *Desire in the Renaissance: Psychoanalysis and Literature.* Princeton, N.J.: Princeton University Press, 1994.

Fumerton, Patricia, and Simon Hunt, eds. *Renaissance Culture and the Everyday*. Philadelphia: University of Pennsylvania Press, 1999.

Halliday, F. E. *Shakespeare in His Age*. South Brunswick, N.J.: Yoseloff, 1965.

Harrison, G. B., ed. *The Elizabethan Journals: Being a Record of Those Things Most Talked of During the Years 1591–1597*. Abridged ed. 2 vols. New York: Doubleday Anchor, 1965.

Harrison, William. *The Description of England: The Classic Contemporary [1577] Account of Tudor Social Life*. Edited by Georges Edelen. Washington, D.C.: Folger Shakespeare Library, 1968. Reprint, New York: Dover, 1994.

Jardine, Lisa. *Reading Shakespeare Historically*. London: Routledge, 1996.
———. *Worldly Goods: A New History of the Renaissance*. London: Macmillan, 1996.

Jeanneret, Michel. *A Feast of Words: Banquets and Table Talk in the Renaissance*. Translated by Jeremy Whiteley and Emma Hughes. Chicago: University of Chicago Press, 1991.

Kernan, Alvin. *Shakespeare, the King's Playwright: Theater in the Stuart Court, 1603–1613*. New Haven and London: Yale University Press, 1995.

Lockyer, Roger. *Tudor and Stuart Britain, 1471–1714*. London: Longmans, 1964.

Rose, Mary Beth, ed. *Renaissance Drama as Cultural History: Essays from Renaissance Drama, 1977–1987*. Evanston, Ill.: Northwestern University Press, 1990.

Schmidgall, Gary. *Shakespeare and the Courtly Aesthetic*. Berkeley: University of California Press, 1981.

Smith, G. Gregory, ed. *Elizabethan Critical Essays*. 2 vols. Oxford: Clarendon Press, 1904.

Tillyard, E. M. W. *The Elizabethan World Picture*. London: Chatto and Windus, 1943. Reprint, Harmondsworth: Penguin, 1963.

Willey, Basil. *The Seventeenth Century Background: Studies in the Thought of the Age in Relation to Poetry and Religion*. New York: Columbia University Press, 1933. Reprint, New York: Doubleday, 1955.

Wilson, F. P. *The Plague in Shakespeare's London*. 2d ed. Oxford: Oxford University Press, 1963.

Wilson, John Dover. *Life in Shakespeare's England: A Book of Elizabethan Prose.* 2d ed. Cambridge: Cambridge University Press, 1913. Reprint, Harmondsworth: Penguin, 1944.

Zimmerman, Susan, and Ronald F. E. Weissman, eds. *Urban Life in the Renaissance.* Newark: University of Delaware Press, 1989.

Dramatic Development

Cohen, Walter. *Drama of a Nation: Public Theater in Renaissance England and Spain.* Ithaca, N.Y.: Cornell University Press, 1985.

Dessen, Alan C. *Shakespeare and the Late Moral Plays.* Lincoln: University of Nebraska Press, 1986.

Fraser, Russell A., and Norman Rabkin, eds. *Drama of the English Renaissance.* 2 vols. Upper Saddle River, N.J.: Prentice Hall, 1976.

Happé, Peter, ed. *Tudor Interludes.* Harmondsworth: Penguin, 1972.

Laroque, François. *Shakespeare's Festive World: Elizabethan Seasonal Entertainment and the Professional Stage.* Translated by Janet Lloyd. Cambridge: Cambridge University Press, 1991.

Norland, Howard B. *Drama in Early Tudor Britain, 1485–1558.* Lincoln: University of Nebraska Press, 1995.

Theater and Stage

Doran, Madeleine. *Endeavors of Art: A Study of Form in Elizabethan Drama.* Milwaukee: University of Wisconsin Press, 1954.

Gibson, Leslie Joy. *Squeaking Cleopatras: The Elizabethan Boy Player.* Stroud, U.K.: Sutton, 2000.

Grene, David. *The Actor in History: Studies in Shakespearean Stage Poetry.* University Park: Pennsylvania State University Press, 1988.

Gurr, Andrew. *Playgoing in Shakespeare's London.* Cambridge: Cambridge University Press, 1987.

———. *The Shakespearian Stage, 1574–1642.* 3d ed. Cambridge: Cambridge University Press, 1992.

Halliday, F. E. *A Shakespeare Companion, 1564–1964.* Rev. ed. Harmondsworth: Penguin, 1964.

Harrison, G. B. *Elizabethan Plays and Players*. Ann Arbor: University of Michigan Press, 1956.

Holmes, Martin. *Shakespeare and His Players*. New York: Scribner, 1972.

Ingram, William. *The Business of Playing: The Beginnings of the Adult Professional Theater in Elizabethan London*. Ithaca, N.Y.: Cornell University Press, 1992.

Kastan, David Scott. *Shakespeare and the Book*. Cambridge: Cambridge University Press, 2001.

LeWinter, Oswald, ed. *Shakespeare in Europe*. Cleveland, Ohio: Meridian, 1963.

Marcus, Leah S. *Unediting the Renaissance: Shakespeare, Marlowe, Milton*. London: Routledge, 1996.

Orgel, Stephen. *The Authentic Shakespeare, and Other Problems of the Early Modern Stage*. New York: Routledge, 2002.

Ornstein, Robert. *A Kingdom for a Stage: The Achievement of Shakespeare's History Plays*. Cambridge, Mass.: Harvard University Press, 1972.

———. *Shakespeare's Comedies: From Roman Farce to Romantic Mystery*. Newark: University of Delaware Press, 1986.

Salgādo, Gāmini. *Eyewitnesses of Shakespeare: First Hand Accounts of Performances, 1590–1890*. New York: Barnes and Noble, 1975.

Stern, Tiffany. *Rehearsal from Shakespeare to Sheridan*. Oxford: Clarendon Press, 2000.

Thomson, Peter. *Shakespeare's Professional Career*. Cambridge: Cambridge University Press, 1992.

Webster, Margaret. *Shakespeare Without Tears*. New York: Whittlesey House, 1942.

Weimann, Robert. *Shakespeare and the Popular Tradition in the Theater: Studies in the Social Dimension of Dramatic Form and Function*. Edited by Robert Schwartz. Baltimore: Johns Hopkins University Press, 1978.

Wikander, Matthew H. *The Play of Truth and State: Historical Drama from Shakespeare to Brecht*. Baltimore: Johns Hopkins University Press, 1986.

Yachnin, Paul. *Stage-Wrights: Shakespeare, Jonson, Middleton, and the*

Making of Theatrical Value. Philadelphia: University of Pennsylvania Press, 1997.

Biography

Halliday, F. E. *The Life of Shakespeare.* Rev. ed. London: Duckworth, 1964.

Honigmann, F. A. J. *Shakespeare: The "Lost Years."* 2d ed. Manchester: Manchester University Press, 1998.

Schoenbaum, Samuel. *Shakespeare's Lives.* New ed. Oxford: Clarendon Press, 1991.

———. *William Shakespeare: A Compact Documentary Life.* Oxford: Oxford University Press, 1977.

Wells, Stanley. *Shakespeare: A Life in Drama.* New York: W. W. Norton, 1995.

General

Bergeron, David M., and Geraldo U. de Sousa. *Shakespeare: A Study and Research Guide.* 3d ed. Lawrence: University of Kansas Press, 1995.

Berryman, John. *Berryman's Shakespeare.* Edited by John Haffenden. Preface by Robert Giroux. New York: Farrar, Straus and Giroux, 1999.

Boyce, Charles. *Shakespeare A to Z: The Essential Reference to His Plays, His Poems, His Life and Times, and More.* New York: Facts on File, 1990.

Bradbey, Anne, ed. *Shakespearian Criticism, 1919–35.* London: Oxford University Press, 1936.

Colie, Rosalie L. *Shakespeare's Living Art.* Princeton, N.J.: Princeton University Press, 1974.

Dean, Leonard F., ed. *Shakespeare: Modern Essays in Criticism.* Rev. ed. New York: Oxford University Press, 1967.

Everett, Barbara. *Young Hamlet: Essays on Shakespeare's Tragedies.* Oxford: Oxford University Press, 1989.

Grene, David. *The Actor in History: A Study in Shakespearean Stage Poetry.* University Park: Pennsylvania State University Press, 1988.

Goddard, Harold C. *The Meaning of Shakespeare.* 2 vols. Chicago: University of Chicago Press, 1951.

Kaufmann, Ralph J. *Elizabethan Drama: Modern Essays in Criticism.* New York: Oxford University Press, 1961.

McDonald, Russ. *The Bedford Companion to Shakespeare: An Introduction with Documents.* Boston: Bedford, 1996.

Raffel, Burton. *How to Read a Poem.* New York: Meridian, 1984.

Ricks, Christopher, ed. *English Drama to 1710.* Rev. ed. Harmondsworth: Sphere, 1987.

Santillana, Giorgio de, and Hertha von Dechend. *Hamlet's Mill: An Essay of Myth and the Frame of Time.* Boston: Godine, 1977.

Siegel, Paul N., ed. *His Infinite Variety: Major Shakespearean Criticism Since Johnson.* Philadelphia: Lippincott, 1964.

Sweeting, Elizabeth J. *Early Tudor Criticism: Linguistic and Literary.* Oxford: Blackwell, 1940.

Taylor, Gary. *Reinventing Shakespeare: A Cultural History, from the Restoration to the Present.* New York: Weidenfeld and Nicholson, 1989.

Van Doren, Mark. *Shakespeare.* New York: Holt, 1939.

Weiss, Theodore. *The Breath of Clowns and Kings: Shakespeare's Early Comedies and Histories.* New York: Atheneum, 1971.

Wells, Stanley, ed. *The Cambridge Companion to Shakespeare Studies.* Cambridge: Cambridge University Press, 1986.